DEATH, MEM
AND DEVIANT SPACES

Emerald Studies in Death and Culture

Series Editors: Ruth Penfold-Mounce, University of York, UK; Julie Rugg, University of York, UK; Jack Denham, York St John University, UK

Editorial Advisory Board: Jacque Lynn Foltyn, National University, USA; Lisa McCormick, University of Edinburgh, UK; Ben Poore, University of York, UK, Melissa Schrift, East Tennessee State University, USA; Kate Woodthorpe, University of Bath, UK

Emerald Studies in Death and Culture provides an outlet for cross-disciplinary exploration of aspects of mortality. The series creates a new forum for the publication of interdisciplinary research that approaches death from a cultural perspective. Published texts will be at the forefront of new ideas, new subjects, new theoretical applications and new explorations of less conventional cultural engagements with death and the dead.

Published titles
Brian Parsons, *The Evolution of the British Funeral Industry in the 20th Century: From Undertaker to Funeral Director*
Ruth Penfold-Mounce, *Death, the Dead and Popular Culture*

Forthcoming titles
Tim Bullamore, *The Art of Obituary Writing*
Racheal Harris, *Meaning and Symbolism in Pet Inspired Memorial Tattoos: Echoes and Imitations of Life*

DEATH, MEMORIALIZATION AND DEVIANT SPACES

BY

MATTHEW SPOKES
JACK DENHAM
BENEDIKT LEHMANN
York St John University, UK

United Kingdom – North America – Japan
India – Malaysia – China

Emerald Publishing Limited
Howard House, Wagon Lane, Bingley BD16 1WA, UK

First edition 2018

Copyright © Matthew Spokes, Jack Denham and
Benedikt Lehmann. Published under exclusive licence.

Reprints and permissions service
Contact: permissions@emeraldinsight.com

No part of this book may be reproduced, stored in a retrieval
system, transmitted in any form or by any means electronic,
mechanical, photocopying, recording or otherwise without
either the prior written permission of the publisher or a licence
permitting restricted copying issued in the UK by The Copyright
Licensing Agency and in the USA by The Copyright Clearance
Center. Any opinions expressed in the chapters are those of the
authors. Whilst Emerald makes every effort to ensure the quality
and accuracy of its content, Emerald makes no representation
implied or otherwise, as to the chapters' suitability and
application and disclaims any warranties, express or implied, to
their use.

British Library Cataloguing in Publication Data
A catalogue record for this book is available from the British
Library

ISBN: 978-1-78756-574-6 (Print)
ISBN: 978-1-78756-571-5 (Online)
ISBN: 978-1-78756-573-9 (Epub)

Printed and bound by CPI Group (UK) Ltd, Croydon, CR0 4YY

ISOQAR certified
Management System,
awarded to Emerald
for adherence to
Environmental
standard
ISO 14001:2004.

Certificate Number 1985
ISO 14001

INVESTOR IN PEOPLE

CONTENTS

List of Figures vii

Introduction 1
I.1. Doing Things with Heritage 3
I.2. Death, Memorialization and Deviant Spaces 7
I.3. Structure 9
    I.3.1. Theatrics 9
    I.3.2. Consumption 10
    I.3.3. Politicization 10
I.4. The Aims of This Book 11

1. **Heritage and Space: Some Theoretical Perspectives** 13
    1.1. Questions of Power and Scale 15
    1.2. Space as Relational, Space as Social 20
    1.3. Turning Back to Lefebvre 22

2. **Theatrics (The Tyburn Gallows, York)** 27
    2.1. Unpacking Lefebvre's Spatial Triad 31
    2.2. Tyburn as a Historically and Topographically Conceived Space 37
    2.3. Tyburn as a Lived Space 48
    2.4. Tyburn as a Perceived Space 57
    2.5. Tyburn as Theatrical Space 65
    2.6. Conclusion 76

3. **Consumption (Number 25 Cromwell Street, Gloucester)** 79
    3.1. Some Context 82
    3.2. Number 25 as Perceived Space 87
    3.3. Number 25 as Conceived Space 88

	3.4.	Number 25 as Lived Space	92
	3.5.	Theatrical Space or Watched Space?	96
	3.6.	Theatrical Space as Contradictory Space	99
	3.7.	The Space of Consumption	102
	3.8.	Conclusion	104
4.	**Politicization (Neumarkt, Dresden)**		107
	4.1.	Dresden's Neumarkt as Conceived Space	109
	4.2.	Dresden's Neumarkt as Perceived Space	115
	4.3.	Spatial Practice and Political Subjectivities	122
	4.4.	Conclusion	126
5.	**Conclusions**		131
	C.1.	Where Next?	136
Bibliography			141
Index			155

LIST OF FIGURES

Chapter 2

Figure 2.1	Tyburn Detail	27
Figure 2.2	Surrounding Woodland, from Tyburn	29
Figure 2.3	Information Board Detail: Floral Tributes	30
Figure 2.4	Lefebvre's Spatial Triad	32
Figure 2.5	Samuel Parson's 1624 Map	40
Figure 2.6	1853 Map of Micklegate Stray	42
Figure 2.7	1853 Map of Micklegate Stray (St. Mary Bishophill Detail)	43
Figure 2.8	1910 Tyburn Map	44
Figure 2.9	1932 Tyburn Map	45
Figure 2.10	2017 Tyburn Map	46
Figure 2.11	Tyburn Information Sign	48
Figure 2.12	Tyburn Site with Bench	49
Figure 2.13	Dick Turpin's Grave	50
Figure 2.14	Three Legged Mare Sign Detail	51
Figure 2.15	Medieval Boundary Stone	52
Figure 2.16	Little Hob Moor Noticeboard	53
Figure 2.17	Cycle Route across Little Hob Moor	53

List of Figures

Figure 2.18 Distance Marker on Tadcaster/Hob Moor Road 54
Figure 2.19 The Hob Stone (left) 55
Figure 2.20 The Plague Stone Plaque 56
Figure 2.21 New Tree Growth at Knavesmire 58
Figure 2.22 Fenced-off Saplings 59
Figure 2.23 Grass Meadow South of Tyburn 60
Figure 2.24 Sign for Dog Walkers 61
Figure 2.25 Path Adjacent to Racecourse 63
Figure 2.26 Path through Woodland Facing North . . . 64
Figure 2.27 Path through Woodland Facing South . . . 65
Figure 2.28 Tributes to the Jacobite Rebels in 2007 . . . 69
Figure 2.29 Tributes to the Jacobite Rebels in 2007 . . . 70
Figure 2.30 John Thornton Memorial Plaque 71
Figure 2.31 Jimmy Corr Memorial Plaque 72
Figure 2.32 Cycle Crossing 73
Figure 2.33 Tyburn from Below 74
Figure 2.34 Tyburn from Below [shade detail] 75
Figure 2.35 Tyburn Reverse Angle 77

INTRODUCTION

The USA has spent much of 2017 in the throes of far-right marches that glorify confederate statues, and violence has sadly been the outcome of a recent example of this in Charlottesville (as of August 2017). James Glaser (2017, p. 1) asks what to do with the oft-glorified 'difficult heritage' symbols of confederate statues during America's recent swing towards the political right, writing: 'do we just toss them into the ash bin of history, purging them as if they never existed'?

The answer to his question is complex and one that acts as a jumping off point for this book. In some instances, it can be a straightforward 'yes'. Sharon Macdonald (2009) has written of the remnants from large-scale, national atrocities and the ways in which they have been systematically destroyed and deleted from history – like swastika-laden ceilings at Nuremburg, Germany. Dark tourism theorists, on the other hand, have considered how these sites can and have been monetised for the financial gain of private interests and national governments alike (see, for example, Braithwaite and Lee, 2006; Sharpley and Stone, 2009; Stone, 2011).

Glaser is asking a question that has become more complicated of late. An increasing media focus on violence and death is turning the spotlight on exponentially greater number of spaces – making it relevant to those who study criminal-celebrity, who have focused on the memorialization of individuals (see, for example, Kooistra, 1989; Hobsbawm, 2001; McCorristine, 2014). His question also calls to mind research in the area of difficult heritage that has traditionally focused on the politics and architecture of large-scale national atrocities, such as this work from Macdonald. But it also brings up theories of dark tourism that have, for over two decades, contributed much to our understanding of the consumption of death as it is experienced in physical places. Lastly, his question is relevant to spatial theorists who are likely to be more interested in the ways in which the 'difficult dead' – our term for the situating of the dead in problematic spaces – manage to hang around, often unwanted, experienced in myriad ways by local communities despite various efforts to turn these sorts of infamous sites into ash.

This book sits at the meeting point of these approaches and in response to the following questions: how can you memorialize the dead and preserve the architecture of the past without enshrining a space for dark tourists to make their own? Or perhaps, in a more capitalistic sense, how can you develop a thriving dark tourist business without sensationalising the event and offending the sensibilities of the community? As they are often inclined, local councils find themselves trying to toss a space into the bin in a way that would put a halt to any sort of consumeristic tourist interest and unwanted media attention. But instead of just thinking about the legacy of some criminal individuals, or analysing the political position of difficult heritage architecture, or critiquing the monetization of the dead – this employs and develops spatial theory alongside these ideas to explore how three scalar case studies can assist us in understanding the memorialization of the difficult dead. Stone (2011, p. 318) has called for such an interdisciplinary approach before, stating that:

> *Dark tourism research has been characterised by a banality that either illustrates deficient conceptual underpinning or provides for limited disciplinary synthesis. Thus, in order to assuage any structural deficiencies in dark tourism as a coherent body of knowledge, I suggest scholars need to transgress traditional disciplinary borders and interests.*

This book, then, is the synthesis of several relevant research areas offered as a way of unpacking questions about deviance, death and memorialization through three escalating case studies: a bench on the site of an old gallows; the space between some terraced housing and a church; and the recreated historic town centre of a German city.

1.1. DOING THINGS WITH HERITAGE

By way of introduction, let us briefly think about what these research areas have offered, starting with 'difficult heritage'. History is rife with examples of difficult heritage being used for political gain. For instance, Nieves considered difficult black heritage in South Africa and the utilisation of places of pain as tools for social justice (Nieves, 2009). This comes after Litter's (2005) paper considering the use of British race heritage as a catalyst for social change and equality (Litter, 2005). The negative connotations of the past and the associated oppressive regimes have long been researched as places for the incitement of reform, commemoration and reorganization. In Hiroshima, Utaka (2009) has argued that the 25-metre high 'A Bomb Dome' is a memorial for the over 100,000 lives lost in the closing stages of World War II, but it is also billed as an international 'peace memorial'. This piece of architecture is a strong symbol of difficult heritage, war crime and suffering. When Auschwitz was first declared a museum by Poland it was, according to Young (2009), an attempt to 'glorify Polish martyrdom' without a single mention of the word 'Jew' throughout the exhibition. This heritage site was manipulated and presented as a place of Polish pain and suffering – difficult heritage again becoming a political tool.

These findings show the power attached to heritage and heritage architecture. This power is in part due to political manipulation through the preservation process but without the sheer scale of exposure that these national atrocities possess, the use of heritage in this way would not be possible. 'The politics of display',[1] then, can refer to the political might of the displays themselves as well as the often heated arguments that resonate around what should be done with a site so closely associated with atrocity in the public consciousness.

Until recently, small-scale local difficult heritages have been relatively immune to political manoeuvre due to this lack of exposure. The late twentieth century has seen a meteoric rise in international media and online communications framing them as material for political debate and allowing them to be studied alongside these national atrocities. Sharon Macdonald dedicated three chapters to 'structures' in her book *Difficult Heritage: Negotiating the Nazi Past in Nuremberg and Beyond* (2009). 'Building Heritage', 'Demolition' and 'Preservation' help us understand the sheer importance of architecture to heritage and the symbolic power attached to buildings for instance. But this symbolic power extends beyond buildings to other material representations of heritage, for example, the 'Arbeit Macht Frei' gate at Auschwitz (Young, 2009). As tourists walk through the concentration camp they are greeted by the infamous sign under which millions greeted death and depravity. The sign still carries this symbolism and evokes powerful emotions in tourists despite the fact that it has been moved and no longer marks the space where victims arrived at Auschwitz nor where any met their death (Young, 2009). For Young, the power in the buildings at Auschwitz is in their disrepair and lack of preservation. Tourists feel the 'raw' experience not mediated by museum information or formalized on-site narratives. In contrast, heritage is negotiated very differently when obscured through layers of sign, information and politics, for example, as can be seen in the Nuremberg Documentation Centre (Macdonald, 2009). Museums, on the other hand, have often been the subject of research into dark tourism with Stone arguing that their position atop the tourism infrastructure of many locales meant that they were some of the 'lightest' dark tourism sites on his spectrum (2006, p. 151).

Modern (read: 'Western') society is awash with these sites of pain (Logan and Reeves, 2009) and violent history, and dark tourism research has offered us interpretations of the popularity and commercial success of these 'black spots' (Rojek, 1993) in recent years and decades. Graham Dann used the phrase 'milking the macabre' to describe Western fascination with – and capitalization of – sites of death and destruction (1994), whereas Seaton preferred 'thanatourism' (1996), but 'dark tourism' has dominated since Foley and Lennon coined the term (1996), encompassing all research into the commercialization of dark places. This research, on the other hand, will contribute quite the opposite – research into the resistance of commercialization in dark spaces. Further, governments are increasingly concerning themselves with resistance strategies as more and more places become the focus of unwanted, unsavoury media attention. Investigation into criminal-celebrity goes some way in explaining our fascination with these sites of pain: key texts here include Duclos and Pingree's *The Werewolf Complex* (1998) and

Mike Presdee's ground-breaking work on the *Carnival of Crime* (2000).

However, both dark tourism and celebrity-criminal schools of thought still address spaces or the people attached to them through the lens of consumption. Research has variously considered the consumer of violent heritage, the 'thanatourist' (Seaton, 1996) or the criminal fan (Jenks and Lorentzen, 1997) and related commercial consequences (Fiske, 1992). Our contention is that there is a theoretical gap in assessing the local negotiations of the said 'black spots' from the point of view of those blighted by their neighbourhood's immortal association with death and suffering. What are the local, non-commercial consequences of violent criminal difficult heritage? What impact does infamous death, and its highly contested memorialization, have on everyday spatial experiences?

Expanding markets of dark tourism have complicated 'difficult heritage' debates as has the proliferation of criminal-celebrity. It is not just places like Hiroshima or Nuremberg that are negotiating the minefield of their own deviant pasts. Large-scale media exposure, and the proliferation of the celebrity-criminal, means that local communities are also finding themselves in the challenging position of managing their deviant pasts. Structures, in general, carry memory without the need for premeditation like Nuremberg. Strange and Kempa (2003) note that Alcatraz, a popular American dark tourist attraction, has a haunting and cruel atmosphere associated with the powerful and imposing structure of the prison sat atop the island, and it is this embedded deviancy and the impact of memorial and anti-memorial that this book will address through three case studies. We will look at the use of space of differing kinds as a way for cities and local authorities to work through difficult heritage, here seen through the application of spatial theory to our case studies of Tyburn (York), Cromwell Street (Gloucester) and Dresden (Germany).

I.2. DEATH, MEMORIALIZATION AND DEVIANT SPACES

'Difficult heritage' has traditionally considered macro cases of national atrocity. Studies into celebrity crime or infamous death have been local, often individualized, case study based. 'Dark tourism' has been studied in both contexts. This research project will develop the concept of 'difficult heritage' by exploring the intersection between local political discourses, media constructions of violent death and, crucially, spaces of memorialization in England and Germany. Where difficult heritage has previously focused on how ' […] a city and a nation deal with a legacy of perpetrating atrocity' (Macdonald, 2009, p. 1), this project will explore the concept at a micro-level. The intention of the project is to understand the interrelationship between the social, spatial, temporal and political contingencies of these localities, with an emphasis on analysing the contested cultural meanings of space and memory in our chosen heritage sites. In doing so, we seek to develop a conceptual toolbox that responds to Harvey's recent concerns (2015) about the lack of scalar thinking in heritage discourses. The sites we have chosen to focus on are unique because of their media coverage (or lack thereof) and their infamous status. With that in mind, the book asks:

- What are the conceptual tools that can help us to understand the relationship between spatial concerns, local (community) consequences and the memorialization of infamous death?

- How do local communities negotiate 'difficult heritage' under these circumstances?

- What is the context for the interplay and conflicting demands of 'difficult heritage', 'dark tourism' and 'memorialization' through space?

In pursuit of answers, this book attempts to do three things. It rearticulates Lefebvrian spatial theory in relation to dissimilar memorial sites; accounts for scale in debates about difficult heritage, including smaller, more intimate negotiations that have presented themselves to local communities (in part due to ever-expanding media coverage of an ever-widening series of deviant events); and does this through the application of theory to three escalating case studies. Ultimately, this book is an opportunity to gauge how spatial approaches to heritage debates around death and memorialization might be constructed as a workable conceptual toolbox.

This book explores ways of thinking about how the dead continue to inhabit space and place, and how this impacts and reflects differing approaches to memorialization. It makes use of Lefebvre's spatial triad as a way of theorizing conflicting agendas in the spaces of infamous death ranging from the State-sponsored execution of thousands of people between the fourteenth and early nineteenth centuries, through the serial murder of up to 30 people in Gloucester in the mid-to-late twentieth century, right up to contemporary protests over the politicization of a site where between 35,000 to 150,000 people were killed in the closing stages of World War II (Taylor, 2008). We have chosen to focus on three deliberately different case studies to effectively test the adaptability of Lefebvrian theory in relation to the memorialization of the difficult dead. In doing so, we draw on three areas of scholarship that are increasingly overlapping; the way in which the state negotiates histories and memorials that are unsavoury or 'difficult' such as war; dark tourism and the fetishization of sites of death and suffering; and the expanding media coverage and celebration of violent deaths and violent people.

I.3. STRUCTURE

This book follows three case studies that can be read separately, but build gradually from one to the other. Through these three, sometimes disjointed cases, we will specifically focus on adapting, enhancing and applying elements from Lefebvre's spatial corpus that are routinely overlooked; while we start with the spatial triad as many have done before (see Chapter 2) we use this as a stepping-off point to consider, among other things, the theatrical nature of Lefebvre's work on the everyday functioning of urban reality under advanced capitalism, or the notion of contradictory space with regard to consumptive practices. After exploring the utility of varying arguments around space as representational or social in the chapter following this one, we take Lefebvre's work forward and apply it to 'theatrics', 'consumption' and 'politicization'.

I.3.1. Theatrics

The first case study, of the Tyburn memorial and associated environs in suburban York, begins by unpacking the three interconnected elements of Lefebvre's spatial triad, as outlined in *The Production of Space* (1991). The case study is explored through ethnographic and photographic data, including historical records, mapping and field notes/photographs from the site, collected across a two-month period (May–June 2017) and articulated in relation to conceived space, lived space and perceived space before developing the lesser-known concept of 'theatrical space' in an effort to capture the unique aspects of the site as a problematic memorial to State-sanctioned execution. In taking this approach, the case study underscores the challenges of putting together a conceptual toolbox in the light of the variety of competing interests and activities undertaken at the site (local government framing, the narratives told by historical societies, the use of the space for leisure activities and the like).

1.3.2. Consumption

Building on the concept of theatrical space, the second case study – of Number 25 Cromwell Street in Gloucester, or rather the space that was formally occupied by that address – explores Lefebvre through consumption and notion of contradictory space. This involves an analysis of the Cromwell Street walkway in Gloucester and argues that theatrical space is particularly useful when considering cases with high level media exposure (in contrast to the low exposure of Tyburn). In using Lefebvre's notion of 'contradictory space', the chapter unpacks the variety of differing interpretations and usages of the space – from mass media to local governments – as a way to theorize conflicting agendas in the memorialization of famous death. This second case study also uses the theoretical groundwork laid in the first, and begins to embed this alongside theories of consumption, dark tourism and difficult heritage as contributing factors to the production of infamous memorial spaces.

1.3.3. Politicization

Working towards reconnecting with the wider debates of difficult heritage and dark tourism, we return to the genesis of much of the work in these fields of study: the aftermath of World War II. How might the spatial triad, or rather our articulation and emphasis on differing aspects of the triad, enable us to connect our conceptual framework of the local with the international? Is that even possible? The third case study, looking at the annual human chain which is used to 'protect' the historic city centre of Dresden against the far right, draws on Lefebvre's spatial triad to think through human agency and imagined space that combines the physical – the city centre – with the political, namely the use of a human chain as a barrier, both tangible and symbolic. This particular space has become a symbolic protest ground for right-wing groups, such as PEGIDA, whose disaffected supporters find their sense of pride and injury confirmed in the historical legacy of this place, and to build on the theoretical framework from the previous chapters complimentary and contrasting theories will be unpacked, to properly test the validity of our adapted Lefebvrian concepts.

While this book has been collaboratively written, each case study has been principally authored by Matthew Spokes (Tyburn), Jack Denham (Cromwell Street) and Benedikt Lehmann (Dresden).

1.4. THE AIMS OF THIS BOOK

The aim of this book is to identify overlaps and posit ways forward for understanding difficult heritage and dark tourism through the prism of spatial theory; to that end, our concluding remarks on the conceptual framework we have underlined in this volume will suggest the points of departure for further research on the intersection between death, spatiality and infamy.

The book takes the unique approach of considering the memorialization of crimes and deaths that communities and councils sometimes do not wish to be remembered by focusing firstly on scale and secondly on lesser-known applications of Lefebvrian theory. The differing case studies introduced here enable us to challenge the variety of difficult heritage and dark tourist spaces that are encountered on an everyday basis, from a bench on an arterial road to a German city centre, and push at the boundaries of theories that can help us illuminate the competing agendas and rationales that operate in these locales from local government decisions to the effects of excessive media exposure.

Ultimately, the three case studies in this book respond to Harvey's (2015) call for a more considered approach to the problems of scale in heritage — which we will explore in detail in the next chapter — and in doing so we show some of the ways in which theoretical notions of space can be developed and applied on a scalar level to better capture the interstitial nature of contested memorializations of deviant space(s).

NOTE

1. See Macdonald, 1998, on the 'politics of preservation'.

CHAPTER 1

HERITAGE AND SPACE: SOME THEORETICAL PERSPECTIVES

To work towards the development of a conceptual toolkit for understanding deviant spaces, death and memorialization, we will move on from our opening discussion of thanatourism to unpack the value of two broad and contested fields of study, namely heritage studies and spatial studies. Instead of reworking historiographies of different schools of thought (see for example, Winter (2014) on heritage and theory and Sheller (2017) on the spatial and mobilities turn), in this chapter we intend to outline a variety of approaches where heritage and space potentially overlap, especially in relation to the issues of scale and how space is constituted, practised, and understood. This chapter will start by thinking through the applicability of the work of Doreen Massey and David Harvey on scale and power before exploring the wider perspectives of relational and socio-spatial scholars; their ideas will lead us into our rationale for returning to, and building upon, Lefebvre's work, with a conclusory outline of those who have recently utilized Lefebvre's spatial triad as we seek to do here.

This review of theoretical approaches can be seen as a composite akin to Deleuze's contested description of an assemblage, in the sense that we are laying out sometimes disparate components in an effort towards understanding and challenging already substantiated 'collective utterances' on heritage and space through the construction of our own 'hodgepodge' (2007, pp. 176–79); this also aligns closely with Strathern's (2005) work on partial connections. Strathern argues that 'not only is there no totality, each part also defines a partisan position' (ibid., p. 39), so in developing our own layout of perspectives, we forward a particular way of thinking about deviant space that can never be fully captured – or indeed entirely articulated! – based on the aspects of Lefebvre's open-ended project outlined in *The Production of Space* (1991).

These assemblages, or partial connections, speak directly to Jessop et al.'s (2008) concerns about 'one-dimensionalism' whereby socio-spatial typologies become increasingly reductive, specifically in taking individualized examples and extrapolating outward. They identify four schools of thought as complicit in this, namely 'territory', 'place', 'scale' and 'network'. Territorial approaches rarely move beyond the level of the state, where ideas are reduced to 'globalization' as a framing device for how we understand cities in particular. Place-based approaches tend to treat spaces as 'discrete, more or less self-contained, more or less self-identical ensembles' (p. 391) which fails to take into account, for instance, how place is intersected and constituted by the issues of scale. Scale and network-centrist ideas suffer from an overreliance on scale-based justifications for all socio-spatial relations in the case of the former and a one-sided emphasis on the rhizomatic and 'frictionless spaces of flows' (ibid.) in the case of the latter – what this shows is that this debate around typology has identified a clustering of approaches that fail to properly account for the holistic nature of spaces. In sum, the challenge for any practical spatial theory is twofold: (1) to avoid adhering unwittingly or otherwise to entrenched typologies and (2) to fully consider the ramifications (both theoretical and empirical) of developing or adapting theories of space and place in relation to our aforementioned interest in scale.

Moving on from this, in the previous chapter, we suggested that difficult heritage offered some useful insights into the relationship between criminal actions, space and history. MacDonald's work (2006), on what she has called 'undesirable' then 'difficult' heritage, initially focuses on differing interpretations of Nuremburg from a space of collectivized hatred to one of military tribunals and then to a tourist attraction. This latter transformation allies this reading of difficult heritage with what Seaton terms thanatourism, whereby people 'travel to a location wholly, or partially, motivated by the desire for actual or symbolic encounters with death, particularly, but not exclusively, violent death' (1996, p. 240). As with our own case studies, which are framed by violent death in some regard, recent applications of these ideas (Knudsen, 2011) combine thanatourism and difficult heritage to see the ways in which people consume spaces where criminal activities have taken place: in a nutshell, individuals or groups of thanatourists visit spaces of difficult heritage as part of cultural consumption.

1.1. QUESTIONS OF POWER AND SCALE

For our particular project, there is the problem of *scale*. As Antze and Lambek (1996, p. 248) highlight, thanatourism can potentially be understood as tourists wanting to be an active part of a *larger history*, something which chimes with

Knudsen's work on Ground Zero and Auschwitz-Birkenau (2011), and MacDonald's work on Nuremburg (2009). However, can the application of concepts related to difficult heritage and thanatourism work *across multiple scales* such as a bench next to an arterial road (Tyburn in York, our first case study), a cut-through between streets in Gloucester (the former site of Fred and Rosemary West's house, our second case study) and a German city centre destroyed in World War II, subsequently rebuilt and now a focal point for new forms of nationalist and counter nationalist protest (Dresden, our third case study)?

This concern speaks to one of Doreen Massey's issues with time−space compression (a term borrowed from David Harvey (1989)), namely the idea that, in the last 30 years, discussions of space have been not only superseded by time, but have also reflected an increasingly complex process of interconnectivity between people and places. She poses the question: 'How, in the face of all this movement and intermixing, can we retain any sense of a local place and its particularity? An (idealized) notion of an era when places were (supposedly) inhabited by coherent and homogeneous communities is set against the current fragmentation and disruption' (2013, p. 146). This gap between supposed solidity and increasing mobility is filled, Massey suggests, by different geometries of power.

Let us think this through in more detail.

For example, if we think about a space Massey uses − the Kilburn High Road − fully unpacking what this space means, how it is constituted, made and remade is impossible without 'bringing into play half the world and a considerable amount of British imperialist history' (1993, p. 65). This clearly relates to the politicized machinations outlined in the previous chapter with regard to sites like Auschwitz as a historical and contemporary space of negotiated and constructed power dynamics, but also means the macro and micro are intimately related. Our first case study of Tyburn in York cannot be understood without thinking through the relationship between the contemporary use of the space – a memorial – and its previous use as a site for state-sponsored execution. How might this also map on to larger spaces such as cities, or small but different spaces such as a small park between terraced housing in Gloucester? Massey goes on to argue (1993, p. 61) that different flows and connections see individuals and social groups arranged in particular ways depending on relations of power and control, namely who is permitted to move and who is not. Again, with regards to our work, this may be contextualized as who is allowed to speak and frame the debate and who is the recipient of particular stories, be they about execution, serial murder or war crimes. Space and social action are interrelated and inseparable, and this cuts across multiple scales.

Massey is of course echoing the work of Michel de Certeau (1984) who argues that spatial production is necessarily framed by power relations. De Certeau argues that how an individual negotiates space is determined by certain tactics employed to assuage or mitigate spatial features, so something as seemingly mundane as walking to work involves the interplay between the designed aspects of the city – the pavements, the streets, the arrangement of buildings and entrances to buildings and so forth – and how individuals move through or adapt to these spaces; what, for example, is jaywalking if it is not the intentional undermining of central planners? While these interventions are individualized, Dourish (2006) argues that it is possible to extrapolate out the interrelationships of scale and the multiple spatialities of people, technology, capital and goods to see a wider picture: the intertwining of scale and the socio-political.

These debates are not really focused on issues of heritage per se – difficult or otherwise – but offered instead as a critique of the excesses of globalization and associated neoliberal doctrine(s) in a spatial sense. As Fuller and Löw (2017, p. 494) identify, a sizeable amount of spatial theory has been used to analyse and critique capitalism and political economy, but – here echoing Jessop, Brenner and Jones – we should not reduce the potency of these insights to one spatial perspective: we will instead focus on the connections between theatrics, consumption and then politicization.

De Certeau's discussion of subversion in socio-spatial production and Massey's work on power geometries can be applied with regards to heritage debates, as shown by David Harvey's (2015) recent interventions around authorized heritage discourses (henceforth AHD). AHD, Harvey suggests, potentially legitimises the sorts of inequalities of power outlined by Massey, so there is a requirement that heritage debates expand and respond to the sorts of concepts of scale which reflect contemporary theoretical shifts at both micro and macro levels (p. 579); in terms of our three case studies, this would facilitate a conceptual toolkit robust enough to unpack the commonalities and differences between a seat and a conurbation.

Harvey, like Jessop et al., sounds a word of caution in navigating this arena, where 'in a world of scalar uncertainty, we must not retreat either towards the warm glow of "localism", or to bland "universal" platitudes of globalisation' (ibid.). A key problem highlighted is a tendency in heritage work to construe space at a national or international level, neatly avoiding the complexity of what scale is and how it organizes and categorizes. He offers the work of Graham, Ashworth and Tonbridge (2000) – who describe heritage as an 'inherently spatial phenomenon' (p. 4) – as a way of thinking through 'how places at various scales acquire identities and the ways in which people identify with places at these scales' (ibid., p. 7) and, in doing so, shows the significance of people at every level of engagement co-creating heritage beyond the dominant narratives of planners and designers; this idea, as we will detail in the following chapters, is a powerful one, reflecting Lefebvre's spatial triad in how space is co-produced and never fully realized.

More vitally, Harvey's work acts as a clarion call for creativity, a position emphasizing how earlier approaches to heritage have become stultified in their failure to respond to the multitude of scales through which heritage is constituted every day. One such example of creative thinking, which predates Harvey's call, would be the work of Andreas Huyssen (1997) who combines research on cities, literature and architecture, to offer both a macro-level reading of space – where cities function at the level of critical discourses among practitioners, planners, philosophers and writers – and a micro-level analysis of, for example, individual buildings and streets in Berlin: Huyssen is especially good at connecting a multitude of disparate examples of structural change to broader trends in cultural consumption, aesthetics and the like, and manages to combine scale, relational and social readings of space to offer an assemblage that avoids some of the pitfalls identified earlier.

With that in mind, Jessop et al.'s central contention that scholars of space fall into particular traps with theoretically informed empirical research leaves us in a quandary about how to develop a practical approach to examining deviant spaces with regard to memorialization. We have already begun discussing this project in relation to power and scale but it is also worth parcelling up the connections between two dominant schools in spatial theory – the relational and the social before we move on to look at the role that Lefebvre's oeuvre will play in helping us along this road.

1.2. SPACE AS RELATIONAL, SPACE AS SOCIAL

Historically, space is *relational*: Durkheim, for example, draws distinctions of space as a way of thinking that it is both culturally specific and representational (Durkheim, 1915, p. 11). More recently than this, Mol and Law describe differentiated spaces as having 'intricate relations. They co-exist' (1994, p. 663) or, as Fuller and Löw suggest, '…elements within space, space itself and multiple spaces are relationally constituted. To conceive of space relationally is to acknowledge complexity. To work with the tools of spatial sociology is to render this complexity manageable' (2017, p. 470). Subsequently, relational complexity, or rather addressing complexity, needs to be factored in to any spatial analysis. All too often space is framed as an absolute, and in challenging this idea through the relationality of space, we are engaging with the reality of what Thrift (2003, p. 95) describes as the 'highly problematic temporary settlements that divide and connect things up into different kinds of collectivities'. These contested arenas of relationality are also *embodied*, so tools used for spatial analysis need to be designed in response to kinaesthetic, aural and visual experiences – the multisensory world – and how these experiences create and interpret space (ibid). Löw and Weidenhaus' argument (2017, p. 557) about relational space runs parallel to Thrift's in outlining how, in addition to the arrangement of social goods and living beings, two things are required to perceive of space as relational:

> *First, an operation of placement of objects in places (spacing), and second, operations of conceptual synthesis and making sense of the relational significance of this spacing in this space. Spaces can always be grasped by way of the question 'Where?' Both the operation of synthesis and spacings are, of*

course, often institutionalized, that is, they are socially pre-structured and shaped by conventions.

Space can, relationally-speaking, be understood as the interplay between an arrangement of objects, people, structures, conventions and institutions. The danger here is that, in suggesting *everything* is spatial in a relational sense, the significance of particular spaces and the way they are constituted is diminished, and in light of the earlier discussion of power dynamics, this would clearly be a foolish approach with regards to contested spaces of the difficult dead in particular.

How then is relational space sociologically important; how is it *social*? As Gieryn argues (2000, p. 482), there is a need for a 'place-sensitive sociology' that avoids thin descriptions in favour of 'an approach to research that uncovers how and when socio-spatiality provides a fundamental category for analysis and a lens through which to "do" sociological research. Space is as vital to sociology as is time' (p. 477). Here, Gieryn is accentuating Simmel's much earlier condition of space as a site for the social production of meaning, whereby our understanding of a space is signified in terms of things, and processes, and the psychological effects henceforth facilitated (1997, p. 138). The spatial is as much a social construction as a relational one, as underlined by Löw and Weidenhaus (and worth quoting at length):

It is not simply the case that everybody spans their own individual space; but rather, the ways spaces are perceived, experienced and remembered, and how people place themselves and their objects is shaped and pre-structured by institutions. Where and how what is stored or built is a social process; this also applies to when objects are experienced as near or far, associated or unconnected and so on, and accordingly synthesized. (2017, p. 557)

Within this, as we have already seen, there is an embodied element that combines the relational and the social: Fuller and Löw suggest that 'the "transformation" of space from that which is absolute into that which is sociologically significant is a process that takes place through bodies (2017, p. 480). De Certeau (1984), as previously discussed, considers movement through space as a bodily function, and Bourdieu (1984) has similarly developed the relationship between space and social structure as one of embodiment. The physicality of the environment and the people in it, shapes, remoulds and facilitates different types of action and interaction, which we subsequently reify through language (Elias, 1978). Bodies are dynamic, flowing, altering entities and the 'placement of bodies in relational space is also dynamic; it generates, reproduces and challenges socio-spatial orders through perception and practice' (Fuller & Löw, 2017 p. 480). The spatial is relational is social is embodied.

A final caveat, to return to Löw and Weidenhaus (2017, pp. 557–8), is that we should not reduce space to the relations, social or otherwise, between objects and subjects, 'rather spaces emerge from triadic relations. Spacing takes place not only according to convention and subjective judgement, but also reciprocally by virtue of subjects dynamically related to each'. Spaces — symbolic or physical — are therefore complex relational and social entities that can be (frequently hierarchically) thought of as scalar, as well as obfuscated by power relations: it is with this in mind that we turn — or rather return — to Lefebvre.

1.3. TURNING BACK TO LEFEBVRE

Lefebvre's concept of spatial relations is famously typified by the triad: we will not be unpacking the triad here as this will be done in the next chapter by way of a practical demonstration of our developmental methodology. However, we should situate our work more broadly in line with a central question of why Lefebvre is still important in terms of spatial theory and, in particular, how his work might help inform particular spaces of deviance and memorialization given what we have just discussed.

Lefebvre's work, as Shields (1999, 2011) identifies, can be organized into three phases. There is his initial post-*Situationniste International* work on how 'the urban' is constituted as the locus of sociality, where the numerous factors that constitute the functioning of capitalism meet (what he terms 'social centrality' (1996)). The second phase, and the focus of much of our developmental framework in this book, is one in which space is produced not just in a physical sense but at the intersection of a variety of cultural meanings and, notably, lived experiences; Lefebvre's approach, intentionally disorganized and purposively left unfinished, circumvents capitalistic methods of control (1991) by facilitating a multitude of possible readings and applications and, as such, can be seen as a valuable ongoing critique of more rigid perspectives such as Castells and Sheridan (1977) who refuse space as a form of protest in favour of it operating simply as one part of the broader machinations that result in wealth accumulation, exploitation and exchange. Lefebvre develops ideas *of* space, rather than texts *on* space, and much of his second-phase work echoes the debates we have outlined already with regards to relationality, sociality and embodiment (another triad!). His third phase, which we will come to in greater detail when drawing the disparate threads of our conceptual toolkit together at the end, returned Lefebvre to his earlier work on the role of the State (2009), the rhythms of the city (2004) and the potential for individuals and collectives to disrupt spatial ordering in response to the socioeconomic ramifications of globalization, a project that complements both Massey and Harvey.

Beyond this outline, two scalar examples – one of a house and one of a city – show how recent applications of Lefebvre's work also demonstrate the ongoing value of his ideas. Fuller (2017) looks at how space is constructed in the development of a residential tower block in Berlin and combines relational spatial thinking with meaning-making insights from Lefebvre. This includes a methodological approach which looks at the representations of space that constitute housing association meetings – with photographic evidence of, for example, a builder's hut and light fittings – used alongside interviews about related issues including installing raised flowerbeds. Fuller combines multiple understandings of relationality in the context of the 'grass-roots' experiences of those involved in the co-construction of this space, thereby detailing the ongoing importance of Lefebvre's notions of space as an interconnected entity that is constantly made/re-made.

Yeoh (2017) reads Lefebvre at a different scale, that of the continuing development of Kuala Lumpur as a 'world-class city'. Yeoh brings together several strands of Lefebvre's thinking, especially how large-scale historical developments in the downtown area of the city, under the auspices of global and neoliberal doctrine, have seen the reshaping of Kuala Lumpur at the expense of those spaces which fall outside of the increasing homogenization of the city – in this case, mobile soup kitchens for the homeless. Essentially, these problematic spaces are being deleted. Yeoh sees this as part of an 'absolute' spatial narrative Lefebvre spent so much time challenging, where the hierarchy of city space framed by global capital imposes meanings and values that do not necessarily map on to the lived experiences of everyday people: he says, 'once a stable buffer, immovable capital as embedded in the built environment of cities has now morphed into a deregulatory site for financialization and neoliberal entrepreneurialism in fictitious capital and credit money' (p. 572). In doing so, Yeoh combines the antagonism of Lefebvre's first phase with his return to a more overt political engagement in his third phase.

These two case studies are diverse in a scalar sense, and in the context of our three case studies, all are either embedded in, or constitute, the 'urban'; aside from showing the power of space in transforming the lives of people – and how people are able to shape space to their own needs even in the context of increasing levels of control – we can also see the continuing vitality of 'thinking through' with Lefebvre, whose work complements Harvey on scale, Massey on power geometry and de Certeau and Thrift on embodiment.

To summarize, our contention is that the flexibility and theoretical rigour of Lefebvre's work, particularly the potentialities of his second-phase writing on spatial production – in tandem with the notion of the 'Right to the City' (Lefebvre, 1996) as a central meeting point for social exchange, action and interaction – combined with our earlier discussion of political economy, relationality, sociality and embodiment – will inform the construction and development of our practical toolkit for understanding memorialization in the context of deviant spaces: again, as we debated in the first chapter, while there has been relevant work done in this area, especially around difficult heritage and dark tourism/thanatourism, there has been little to no emphasis on the scalar relations between criminal sites and how, formally or informally, individually or collectively, they are thought of, memorialized or forgotten. Lefebvre's open-ended invitation to engage affords us the opportunity to explore, through our three case studies, how the interconnected theories might be put to use or developed in this field, moving closer to Waterton and Watson's (2013) call for a 'critical imagination' in the study of heritage.

CHAPTER 2

THEATRICS (THE TYBURN GALLOWS, YORK)

Figure 2.1. Tyburn Detail

Copyright Matthew Spokes

> *Cold breath in the air, a spring chill, sun diffusing through the leaves and branches of an old horse chestnut, positioned directly in front of the steps.*

> *Between 8.20 and 8.30, 70 school children pass through the site. The path forks directly in front and they all head left down on to the racecourse. How can you age a tree by measuring the trunk? An inch a year? A nursery school walks past with about 30 kids and lots of helpers. Older kids on bikes leant against the fence. Dog walkers crossing right to left outside of the wooded space.*
>
> *Man in shorts and short-sleeved shirt without a dog turns and walks towards me, doubling across having missed the path. He then doubles back again and walks away. Odd. Traffic behind very loud, people walking to work, all heading north. Dog walker eyes me suspiciously as she downs the steps. Dog stays with me a while, then trots off. The caws of crows in nearby trees; they're nesting in the dead branches.*

This opening vignette, a snapshot of my initial field notes, captures part of the complicated arrangement of people, objects and spaces present at York's 'Tyburn', or 'without Micklegate Bar' or even just 'Knavesmire' as it is known in some historical records (Knipe, 1867). Living on the outskirts of York, I cycle past Tyburn twice daily, caught in what Lefebvre (2004) calls the linear rhythms of industrialized space–time, and like many people I gave it almost no mind because there is relatively little to it as a memorial site: some concrete slabs, two benches facing down a slope into mature woodland (Figure 2.2), a small flight of stairs heading in the same direction and a stone block with the word 'Tyburn' carved into the surface (Figure 2.1). There is also a noticeboard installed by the York City Council in conjunction with a local historical group – Dringhouses and Woodthorpe –

Figure 2.2. Surrounding Woodland, from Tyburn

Copyright Matthew Spokes

who are responsible for the short biography of the space and what it was once used for. The board includes details of 'rebellious Scots' put to death and a brief sketch of Dick Turpin, as well as showing some of the floral tributes left at the site (Figure 2.3). Over the duration of my field work, I started by seeing a small bundle of sticks wrapped up with a ribbon, but over time, these were added to with three bunches of flowers.

In this chapter, I am going to do two things. Firstly, I am going to think through the ongoing memorialization of Tyburn using Lefebvre's spatial triad (1991) as a methodological tool for unpacking and exploring deviant spaces: here I am framing Tyburn as deviant in relation to both the use of the space as somewhere where criminals were executed, but also as a space that represents State-sponsored violence

Figure 2.3. Information Board Detail: Floral Tributes

Copyright Matthew Spokes

against its citizens. Secondly, building on Lefebvre's associated concepts, I will move on to consider the value of the 'theatrical space' in understanding the ongoing intersections, interferences and interdependencies that facilitate this particular site of memorialization, reflecting the confluence of representational and social space highlighted in the previous chapter.

The data involved in this case study are predominantly visual documents (photographs), field notes (charting my experiences and initial analytical considerations of the space) as well as contemporary and historical documents. Using these data, I will show how time and space can be understood in part through the relational triad of spatial practice, representations of space and representational spaces. Essentially, I will argue that by considering the specific role(s) of Tyburn as a place of execution, both historically and contemporaneously, the notion of 'theatrical space' effectively augments and builds upon the spatial triad, offering a more nuanced understanding of the liminality and multifarious contexts of problematic deviant memorialization.

My approach is to offer, in the first instance, an introduction to Lefebvre's spatial triad by detailing the three interrelated aspects of his spatiotemporal world as laid out in *The Production of Space* (1991); secondly, I will consider Tyburn in relation to each of the components of this triad. Thirdly, I will suggest how, by adapting and applying Lefebvre's notion of theatrical space, we can undercut practical difficulties with the triad so as to present a conceptual framework which reflects the contested nature of deviant spaces, such as those associated with death, dying and – in this particular case – execution. In attempting to develop a toolkit for this type of space, I intend to demonstrate the applicability of Lefebvre one a relatively micro scale – one historical site – which will then leave breathing room for my co-authors to develop this further at other scales, in response to Harvey's call in the previous chapter, for a more robust engagement with the scalar nature of heritage space.

2.1. UNPACKING LEFEBVRE'S SPATIAL TRIAD

As discussed in Chapter 2, Lefebvre's work on space is extensive, diverse and ultimately unfinished (albeit intentionally), but his definitions are built on a foundation where '[...] social space [is] multifaceted: abstract and practical, immediate and mediated' (1991 p. 266). Space is not simply a physical arrangement of objects, but is also the complex interplay of abstract and practical ideas, people and physical structures. He explains that the production of space involves a

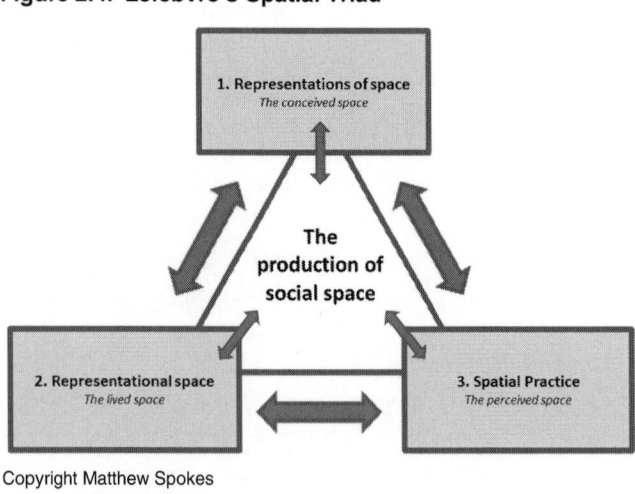

Figure 2.4. Lefebvre's Spatial Triad

```
                1. Representations of space
                    The conceived space

                          ↕
                        The
                    production of
                    social space
                    ↗           ↖
2. Representational space          3. Spatial Practice
     The lived space   ←→           The perceived space
```

Copyright Matthew Spokes

combination of representations of space (*espace conçu* or space as it is conceived), representational space (*espace vécu* or space as it lived in a symbolic sense) and spatial practices (*espace perçu* or the everyday life of spaces). Figure 2.4 shows the arrangement and relationship of these three aspects of spatial production.

Brenner and Elden (in Lefebvre, 2009) suggest that Lefebvre's earlier preoccupations with space are bound up in a Marxist dialectic on the State, where hierarchical territories of space were imposed from above, and the development and eventual consensual understanding of various institutions was denied sociality through the imposition of a 'system of "adapted" expectations and responses' (p. 225); as such, productive social change is curtailed in these spaces (Lefebvre lists families, schools and workplaces as potential examples where social production may be restricted by institutional frameworks). In relation to Tyburn, we might consider a similar range of 'adapted expectations and responses', where social activity – the act of execution, spectatorship, the current use of the space as a memorial – produces a range of actions and reactions. The suggestion of hierarchy in this early definition, where lived experience is predicated by institutional form, also suggests that space, in its multifaceted configurations, is controlled through a variety of means; in Lefebvre's early work, control is largely institutional, but in *The Production of Space* (1991) this is extended to broader notions of sociality:

> *Social space may be described and explained, at least partially, in terms of an intentional signifying process, in terms of sequential or stratified codes and in terms of imbricate forms. Dialectical movements 'superclassify' and 'supercode' overlapping categorizations and logical connections. (p. 233)*

Sociality and dialogue are interconnected processes, with spatiality understood in terms of the sorts of codes and classifications that enable us to interpret physicality (our bodies movement in space for instance), expectation (how we think our interactions will be met) and permission (who can move and who cannot) within a given context. These processes may be 'conceived' – that is, partially controlled by dominant forces – or 'lived', so challenged by lived experience, or interactions with signs, symbols and art (pp. 33–34). Both are impacted by our everyday use and engagement with space and spatial practice: in relation to Tyburn, it is important to fully unpack the nature of the triadic relationships Lefebvre develops so as to properly ascertain their applicability and test their limitations in a practical sense.

The first of the concepts in the spatial triad – conceived space or representations of space – is 'conceptualized space, the space of scientists, planners, urbanists, technocratic subdividers and social engineers' who 'identify what is lived and what is perceived with what is conceived'; this is the 'dominant space in any society (or mode of production)' (Lefebvre, 1991, p. 33). This space takes on a physical form embodied in maps, designs and models, but is – as Gronlund (1993) suggests – essentially 'peopleless'. Lefebvre states that these spaces are where the history of ideologies resides (1991, p. 116), and features that are emphasized in these spaces over time demonstrate the dominant ideologies of a particular epoch: these spaces, through constructed representations of the built environment that may map on to actual, physical structures, embed particular ideas within the texture of a locality (p. 42), thereby demonstrating how thoughts and designs can become actions (Lefebvre, 2000a). As Lefebvre (1991, p. 222) concludes, a '[…] conceived space is a place for the practices of social and political power; in essence, it is these spaces that are designed to manipulate those who exist within them'.

Lived space – the representational – is 'space as directly lived through its associated images and symbols, and hence the space of "inhabitants" and "users"' (p. 33). Lefebvre's notion of thought (2000b, p. 135) can be understood as analogous to the lived space of the representational, which sits atop the physical arrangement of objects and offers a symbolic use and interpretive framework for interpreting said objects. These symbolic engagements are also historically constituted – Lefebvre's example is the use of protest slogans in the May 1968 uprising in Paris (1991 p. 48) – which is why a historical reading of space is foregrounded in the triad, but these symbols are not necessarily cohesive in the way that the maps and plans of conceived space are. Instead, lived space allows for the development of ideas *in relation to* the physical.

The third type of space – the perceived – 'embraces production and reproduction, and the particular locations and spatial sets characteristic of each social formation' (1991, p. 33). Connected to the aforementioned Marxist antagonism against the State, Lefebvre posits that spatial practices under capitalism involve deciphering what representations of space and the representational might mean in relation to the everyday experiences of coexisting in these sorts of locales. This means that perceived space is *bifurcated* space, always related but separating out into what he terms 'urban reality' and 'daily reality': the former can be thought of as the networks and routes that connect private space, work space and leisure space, whereas the latter relates to everyday routines (Lefebvre, 1991, p. 38). This dichotomy demonstrates both the routinization of spatial engagement – both conform to particular relations that repeat in some sort of order such as walking the dog every morning or taking the bus home from work – but also the potential for the illogical: just because we think we understand a particular space because we move through it or interact with it regularly does not mean we know it in its totality of relations.

To return to my own example, Tyburn, as a space on the fringes of an arterial road in and out of the city, contains elements of these spatial entanglements: it is a space where people were once executed, that is historically constituted (reinforced by maps and the work of local history groups) but now appears at first glance to be used as a space of transit. What we see with perceived space are the ways in which the spatiotemporality of conceived and lived space (representations and the representational) are transformed through social activity, or the social production of space (Lefebvre, 1991, p. 117), constituting the 'practical basis of the perception of the outside world'.

It would be tempting, having delineated the spatial triad, to presume that it can be overlaid in a relatively straightforward manner, but Lefebvre also urges caution in this respect and it is worth quoting at length:

> *Knowledge of spaces wavers between description and dissection. Things in space, or pieces of space, are described. Part-spaces are carved out for inspection from social space as a whole. Thus we are offered a geographical space, an ethnological space, a demographic space, a space peculiar to the information sciences, and so on ad infinitum. Elsewhere we hear of pictural, musical or plastic spaces. What is always overlooked is the fact that this sort of fragmentation tallies not only with the tendency of language itself, not only with the wishes of specialists of all kinds, but also with the goals of existing society, which, within the overall framework of a strictly controlled and thus homogeneous totality, splits itself up into the most heterogeneous spaces: housing, labour, leisure, sport, tourism, astronautics, and so on. (1991, p. 91)*

By imposing categorisation, he suggests that we are delimiting the complex and interwoven realities of space. This is clearly problematic if left unaddressed, but at the same time exploring Tyburn and grasping its many meanings will not be possible without some sort of descriptive clarity; endeavouring to balance these approaches and concerns is vital. With this in mind, although I will be separating out the three prongs of the triad in the proceeding sections, interrelationality will be foregrounded, and the broader notions of spatial associations will be challenged through the adaptation of part of Lefebvre's larger corpus on space, particularly the notion of 'theatrical space'. My argument then is that while the spatial triad offers a useful starting point for our analysis in this book, the issue of liminality in contested spaces – the less-than-tangible nature of deviant places of heritage in transition – needs to be explored and that by modifying Lefebvre's ideas around intersectionality in theatrical space, we might move closer to a workable approach that enables researchers to understand deviant and infamous space while preserving some of the intangibility that is often lost when codifying our spatial experiences in this way.

2.2. TYBURN AS A HISTORICALLY AND TOPOGRAPHICALLY CONCEIVED SPACE

Having started to unpack Lefebvre's spatial triad, I will first consider conceived space – or representations of space – through the ways in which Tyburn has been historically and topographically represented.

On the 31 March 1379, Edward Hewison, a native of Stockton and a private solider in the Earl of Northumberland's Light Horses, was the first man to be executed at Tyburn, having been convicted of the rape of 22-year-old Louise Bently, a servant from the nearby castle at Sheriff Hutton. Hewison had been taken from his quarters on Pavement in York to the Castle: from here he was transported by cart up along Micklegate, under the forbidding bar, and south towards the city limits at Little Hob Moor. Following his execution, his body was hanged from a gibbet in the field where the crime had been committed, to the north of the city around about where the River Foss crosses through the village of Strensall today.

On the 29 August 1801, another Edward (Hughes) was also convicted of rape – of Mary Brown, a resident of Tollerton near Easingwold. He was a soldier and was also executed at Tyburn, the last to take place before the gallows were moved inside the Castle[1] so as to prevent the spectacle of the procession of the condemned through the streets to their deaths. These two executions, separated by over 400 years, effectively bookend the working life of Tyburn as a site of city and county execution on the outskirts of York, a space now occupied by a relatively non-descript plaque near a cycle crossing on one of the primary arterial roads in and out of the city.

The gallows at Tyburn – named after the execution site in Middlesex – were commissioned by the Lord Mayor in 1379 to replace the gibbet previously occupying the site on the outskirts of York. This site corresponds to what has been termed the 'importance of visibility' in relation to the confluence of the condemned body, the landscape and potential public interest generated by the execution/executed (see Tarlow and Dyndor, 2015). Tyburn, and the gibbet there before it, sits on a glacial deposit that elevates the space in relation to the surrounding area, as well as being situated next to a road that has served as the main access point to York since Constantine the Great was on the throne. With regard to public interest, as stated in *The True and Illustrated Chronicles of the Last Man Gibbetted in Yorkshire* (Broughton, 1900), crowds of up to 40,000 people could be expected to attend executions and gibbetting, the most notable case at Tyburn being the execution of Dick Turpin in 1739, where crowds stretched a mile from the city walls at Micklegate to the gallows along the road the highwayman was paraded through.

The variety of offences you could be executed for at Tyburn is vast, in line with much of the rest of England before the eventual dismantling of the gallows in 1812 (Herrup, 1989), and included 'being a gipsy', being a 'dangerous person', 'using charms' and 'being suspicious'. In terms of the execution itself, alongside the short-drop three-legged mare gallows,[2] which allowed the convicted to swing for hours on end after choking to death, you could have your head cut off for display on the city bars (gates) or, in the case of those involved in the Jacobite rebellion of 1745, have your heart cut out and thrown into a fire set in front of the baying crowds (Knipe, 1867). If you were to be put to death at Tyburn, you might also be met by tens of thousands of onlookers, with executions routinely scheduled against race meetings to ensure maximum exposure. In relation to the power structures and dominant ideologies that Lefebvre refers to in his assessment of conceived space, this of course corresponds to Foucault's (1977) discussion of the role that bodily punishment played in asserting the control of the monarch, exemplified in their power over life and death through the functionaries and institutions of the State. The number of punishments for what we would, in a contemporary sense, consider minor offences reinforces the power hierarchy that dominated this time in history. In textual accounts such as Knipe's (1867), and in relation to what Tarlow and Dyndor (2015) discuss as the visibility of power manifest in tactical positioning of the space of death, Tyburn spends 422 years as a functional space of death, of spectacle, for an audience, be you a passer-by entering the city or a genuine local spectator.

It is also possible to see how conceived space can be understood in a topographical sense by looking at documentary evidence from historical maps, in line with Lefebvre's space for planners, designers and architects (1991); this space was built with a purpose, so here I am considering how Tyburn is constituted through these representations, and how the nature of the space changes over time.

The earliest surviving map of the area around Tyburn is Samuel Parson's *The Plott of the Mannor of Dringhouses Lyinge within the Countie of the Cittie of Yorke* (Figure 2.5).

Figure 2.5. Samuel Parson's 1624 Map

York Archives

The map, produced in 1624 — some 300 years after the establishment of the gallows at Tyburn — faces south to north, rather than north to south, and shows strip field systems alongside what is now Tadcaster Road. Tyburn is just to the south of the strip fields, showing that between the fifteenth and eighteenth centuries the space where Tyburn is situated was part of common land on the outskirts of the city. It also shows how this space has been framed in relation to the ongoing dispute between occupants and the State as part of the parliamentary Inclosure Acts, and this is further depicted in John Lunds' map from 1772 (not reproduced here); Tyburn is a fringe space, used *by* the city but not *of* the city, evidenced in the spread of an agricultural system that between 1604 and 1914 is eventually outlawed by the State so as to make common land private, a further demonstration of the ideological apparatus of control over the rights of inhabitants to utilize the space (Clark and Clark, 2001).

The first accessible map produced after the dismantling of the gallows in 1812 is the 1853 Ordnance Survey map of York (Ordnance Survey 1853), the details of which can be seen in Figures 2.6 and 2.7. These maps show that by the mid-nineteenth century, agricultural common land has been replaced by the railway and brick works – visible to the left of the map below Hob Moor Lane – and a number of large residential developments: this echoes the increasing co-opting of former public land to enable the development of private interests. Figure 2.6 shows the White House estate to the north of the Tyburn site, and Figure 2.7 shows more detail of the Mount Villas development in St. Mary Bishophill. These residential spaces show how the southward expansion of York along Tadcaster Road moves closer to meeting with the then village of Dringhouses (the area is now an outer suburb of York adjacent to other medieval villages like Acomb), with this expansion facilitated by the compulsory confiscation of common land.

By 1910 (Figure 2.8), the expansion of residential dwellings is even more pronounced, with the St. George's Place houses built to the north of the White House estate, the Mount Villas area considerably expanded (the clay pits by this stage are closed, and by 1932 (Figure 2.9) filled in for the expansion of the railway sidings) and the South Bank estate built to the north east of the Knavesmire Racecourse.

What these maps show, aside from the shift from agrarian space to residential and leisure space, is that the area directly surrounding Tyburn changes to woodland between 1853 and 1910. The contemporary map of Tyburn (Figure 2.10) shows the same woodland and the same tree-lined roads around the race course extending to the south east of the gallows site: the material features of the site on the eastern side of Tadcaster

42   Death, Memorialization and Deviant Spaces

Figure 2.6. 1853 Map of Micklegate Stray

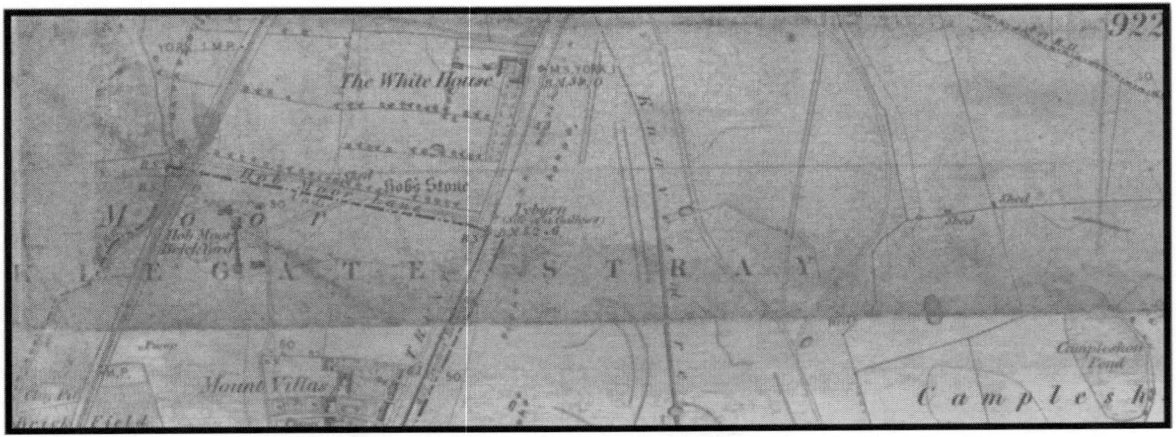

Original © Ordnance Survey 1853

Theatrics (The Tyburn Gallows, York) 43

Figure 2.7. 1853 Map of Micklegate Stray (St. Mary Bishophill Detail)

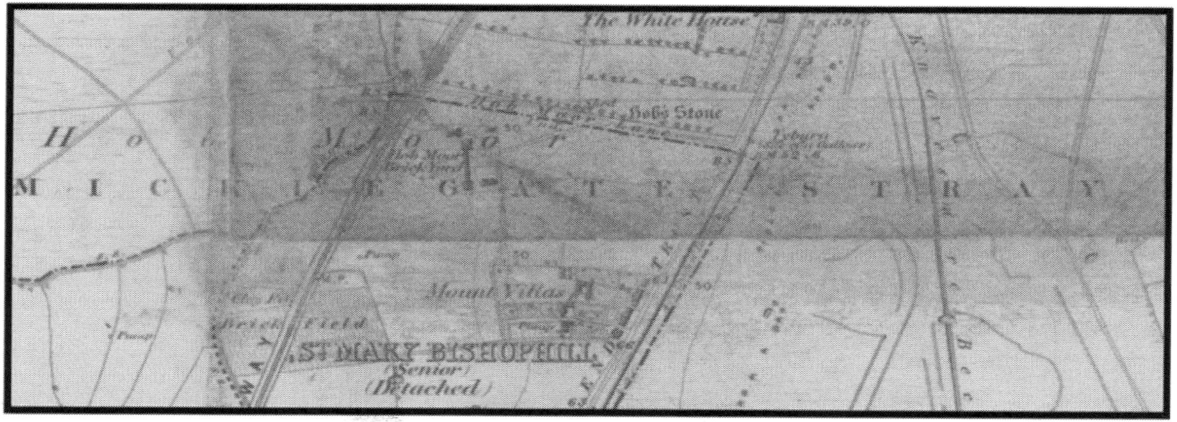

Original © Ordnance Survey 1853

44 Death, Memorialization and Deviant Spaces

Figure 2.8. 1910 Tyburn Map

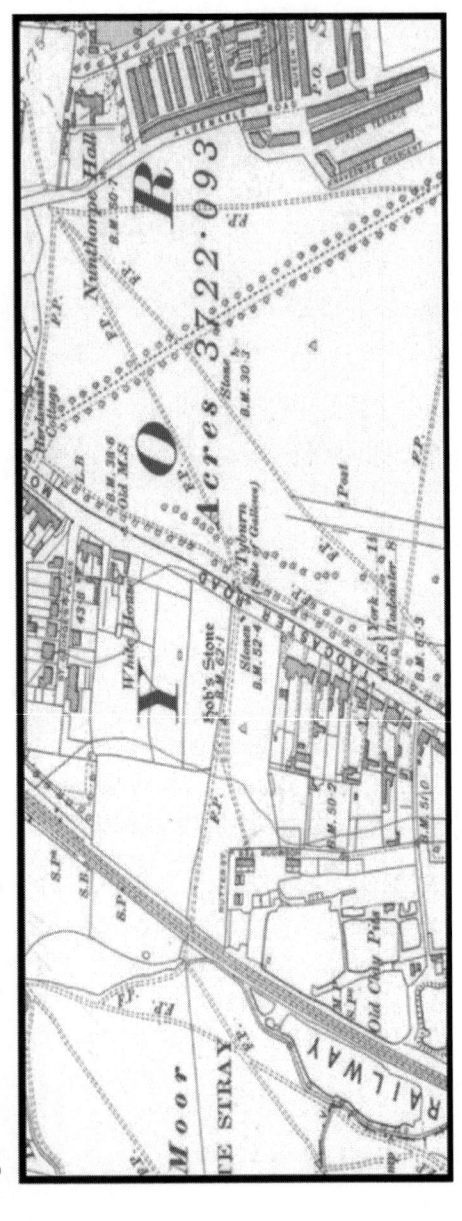

Original © Ordnance Survey 1910

Theatrics (The Tyburn Gallows, York) 45

Figure 2.9. 1932 Tyburn Map

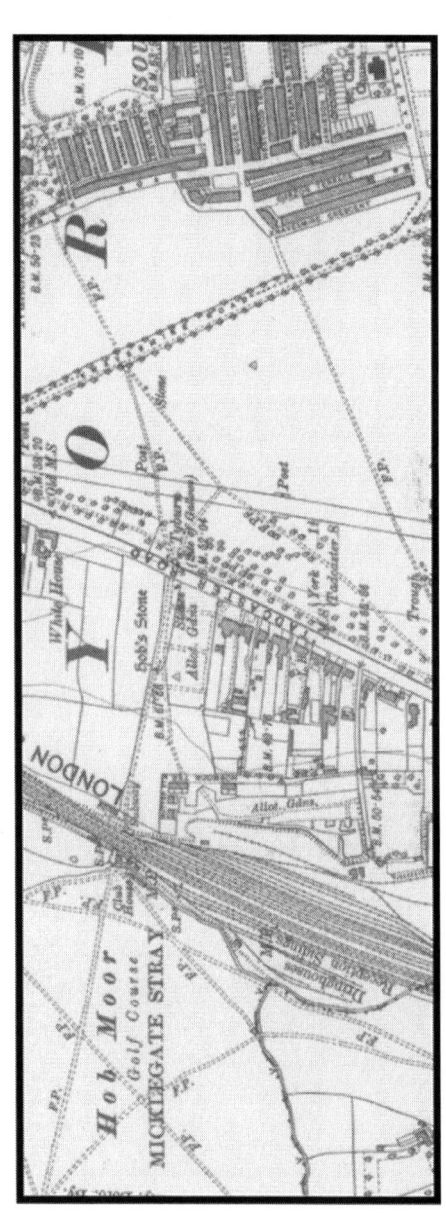

Original © Ordnance Survey 1932

46   Death, Memorialization and Deviant Spaces

Figure 2.10. 2017 Tyburn Map

© Openstreetmap.org Contributors 2017 under Open Database License

Road have, as such, not changed in over 100 years. Today, the northern and western areas surrounding the site are considerably more built up than in 1932, with new housing estates along Pulleyn Drive (the former site of the White House) and Chalfonts (where Mount Villas were previously), and the old chalk pits and railway sidings replaced by housing.

Where Tyburn was once on the outskirts of medieval city, the expansion of the city – in this conceived space – has incorporated Tyburn in to residential areas flanked by woodland to the south east. As such, Tyburn still appears to operate, topologically at least, as a fringe space, but now between residential space and the leisure space of the racecourse. Tyburn is depicted as existing in amongst a changed spatial dynamic, still prominently positioned on a glacial deposit, but hidden by trees from the racecourse – the former site of spectacle. It is no longer the first thing that visitors to the city will see.

The reason this journey through history and topography is important is because it offers documentary-based evidence of the changing nature of the codification of conceived space, how for example the space is now defined in relation to developments that have taken place around it: it is no longer a focal point, but rather a space of memorialization that has been subsumed by the growth of trees, the growth of the city. Evidence of the increasing marginalisation of this deviant space can be seen in the gradual disrepair of the site that led to a newspaper campaign to restore it (Bottomley, 2010), with the local ward committee able to raise £1,500 to restore a bench and the information board at the site (see Figure 2.11 and Figure 2.12).

To return to Lefebvre's opening assertion about the production of space, I have tried to show how these historical and topographical associations correspond to the abstract – the execution of hundreds of men and women across 400 years – and the practical, in the siting of the gallows and

Figure 2.11. Tyburn Information Sign

Copyright Matthew Spokes

potentially the contemporaneous low key memorialization at the site. However, this is only one aspect of the spatial triad and, as suggested earlier, we can begin to see in the latter evidence of the refurbishment of the site and the stories that have been depicted on the information sign (Figure 2.11) how symbolic associations are also used in conjunction with conceived. It is to these symbolic associations — the lived space — that I turn to in the next section.

2.3. TYBURN AS A LIVED SPACE

The previous section focused on Tyburn in terms of how it has been represented, or constituted and framed by planners in relation to historical changes to the space over time. Now

Figure 2.12. Tyburn Site with Bench

Copyright Matthew Spokes

while it is possible to delineate this as being purely a representation of space – the designed element of what a space is supposed to mean – the very nature of what took place at Tyburn problematises these associations, in the same way introduced at the beginning of this book on the issue of difficult heritage (MacDonald, 2009). In this section, I will reflect on the data I collected at the site in May–June of 2017, and how this relates to the idea of *lived* memorialization, thereby demonstrating the representational aspects of Tyburn and what this might mean in a contemporary setting.

Firstly, it is useful to outline the broader associations of Tyburn in relation to the symbolic representations within the city, seeing as York is a tourist destination that trades – in part at least — on its historical connections to grisly crimes.[3] The multitude of 'ghost' and 'murder' tours around York do not feature Tyburn as part of their itineraries, presumably as a result of the distance from the city centre. There are some reminders of the space that can be found within the city however — in relation to the preservation of folk representations of the role the site once played, seen in Dick Turpin's gravestone in St. George's Churchyard (Figure 2.13) and the public house The Three Legged Mare (Figure 2.14) — but generally speaking the space is now a static memorial, rather than one practised through the sort of active heritage associated with York's tourist economy.

That is not to say that the Tyburn site is not connected — through associated symbols — with the history discussed in the previous section. There are a number of ways in which

Figure 2.13. Dick Turpin's Grave

Copyright Matthew Spokes

Figure 2.14. Three Legged Mare Sign Detail

Copyright Matthew Spokes

lived space is framed, or 'dominated – and hence passively experienced' as Lefebvre states (1991, p. 39). Tyburn is flanked to the south and west by two markers that connect it, broadly speaking, with a larger heritage project: in a city such as York, occupied since Roman times, remnants of multiple past iterations litter the landscape. Figure 2.15 is of a mediaeval boundary stone, in this case one delimiting the city (the two benches at Tyburn are just visible to the upper right of the stone). This is a physical reminder of the past, but is also simply present in the landscape: it is not practised heritage, but rather an example of an artefact that remains.

To the west of Tyburn, across Tadcaster Road, the information board for Little Hob Moor – the traditional city

Figure 2.15. Medieval Boundary Stone

Copyright Matthew Spokes

limit – ties in the contemporary nature of heritage in this location more clearly. The board (Figure 2.16) is positioned directly opposite the Tyburn board over the road and offers information on both historical nature of the space and its contemporary usage as an allotment, cycle route and nature reserve (the latter examples are only tacit at Tyburn, which will be discussed in the next section). Another section details on the upcoming events – including history walks – and I have also witnessed this particular space being used for cycle safety awareness programmes. This space is framed as both historical and contemporary. The contemporary cuts through the space both physically (Figure 2.17 shows the cycle route that bisects the space) and symbolically by

Theatrics (The Tyburn Gallows, York) 53

Figure 2.16. Little Hob Moor Noticeboard

Copyright Matthew Spokes

Figure 2.17. Cycle Route across Little Hob Moor

Copyright Matthew Spokes

Figure 2.18. Distance Marker on Tadcaster/Hob Moor Road

Copyright Matthew Spokes

offering markers that demonstrate the transit use of the space (Figure 2.18 shows the distance markers of the road).

The historical association is somewhat downplayed at Little Hob Moor, potentially reflecting the symbolic power of the deviant space of Tyburn in a comparative sense. Little Hob Moor features a stone effigy of a Knight of the Roos family (to the left in Figures 2.19 and 2.20) and is known as the Hob Stone. It was carved in 1315 (prior to the erection of the gallows) but was moved to its present position in 1717, again reinforcing this as a boundary space when considered in tandem with the aforementioned boundary stone (Figure 2.15).

Figure 2.19. The Hob Stone (left)

Copyright Matthew Spokes

The plague stone (Figure 2.20) to the right of the Hobstone was used by plague victims around 1604. They were housed in the area and bought food from locals by placing money in the indented stone (which was filled with vinegar). Symbolically then, this further solidifies the notion that the space in and around Tyburn is for people considered Other from the rest of society. In a historical context, this involved the physical displacement of plague victims to the site adjacent to the gallows – in essence, the State underlining that they are 'as good as dead' – and in a contemporary sense this highlights the spatial distinction between what things were once like (a fringe space on the outskirts of a developing city) and how that contrasts with today (an orbital cycle route in and around the city, through spaces that were once villages separated from York such as Acomb).

Figure 2.20. The Plague Stone Plaque

Copyright Matthew Spokes

It is also worth highlighting, as Lefebvre's spatial triad suggests, the interrelationship between the symbolic/lived and the conceived spaces around Tyburn. The information and notice boards discussed above are also accompanied by maps which delineate spatial usage. In the case of Little Hob Moor, the notice board that contains events information also shows the limits of the space with a thick black line around the perimeter, alongside a key showing usage (allotments, cycle track and the like): in combination with the historical information and the details of the nature reserve, the symbolic function of this is to reinforce dominant usage, while simultaneously offering a reference to the historical significance of the area.

For Tyburn, this is less obvious, as there is no formalized spatial information at the site. However, to the south of Tyburn where the Knavesmire Wood meets Tadcaster Road, there is substantial sign again outlining the different spaces of the site across three maps. One is an amended satellite image showing the wooded space, whereas the others show the broader limits and cycle routes around Knavesmire Racecourse, which is still listed as common land (Micklegate Stray). The effect of these maps side-by-side is that the Tyburn site is symbolically associated not through its history – which is essentially confined to the other noticeboard at the site (Figure 2.11) – but in relation to the established patterns of movement and rights-of-way such as the cycle route.

To return to Lefebvre, what these maps do is provide the interpretive frame for the objects that symbolically relate to Tyburn and its surrounding environs. These maps tie in with the earlier associations of conceived space in terms of the development of residential land, with the networks and pathways – the cycle lines, the road – demonstrating the infrastructural elements of the city rubbing up against the historical spaces that were formerly on the fringes of York.

2.4. TYBURN AS A PERCEIVED SPACE

The third element of Lefebvre's spatial triad involves the spatial practices that take place within a 'perceived space': to reiterate, perceived space is bifurcated space, separating out into 'urban reality' and 'daily reality': the former can be thought of as the networks and routes that connect private space, work space and leisure space, whereas the latter relates to everyday routines (1991, p. 38). In conjunction with the photographic data reproduced in this chapter, an observational analysis of my field notes shows that there are three ways in which Tyburn is utilized as a perceived space: as situated within managed woodland, as a space for dog walkers and as a space of transit for workers.

As previously discussed, the memorial to Tyburn is situated within a mature woodland that runs alongside a main road into York. The woodland was planted sometime after the removal of common land rights in the area, and after the dismantling of the gallows in 1812: it appears on the 1853 map but not on the Lund's Inclosures Act map of 1772. The woodland itself is clearly a carefully managed space, worked on in part by the Woodland Trust whose regional offices are located to the west of the wood. Figures 2.21 and 2.22 show the planting of new saplings – protected and supported by fencing – in the space to complement the existing planting (predominantly horse chestnut trees, including a very large specimen directly opposite the Tyburn memorial); during winter the long grass beneath the trees, which has been allowed to grow freely, is mowed for silage.

Figure 2.21. New Tree Growth at Knavesmire

Copyright Matthew Spokes

Figure 2.22. Fenced-off Saplings

Copyright Matthew Spokes

In addition to this, the area to the east of Tyburn where the trees thin before meeting the racecourse enclosure, wildflower meadows have been planted to encourage wildlife and effectively separate dense woodland from grassland around the racecourse (Figure 2.23). These differing environments demonstrate a mixed-use site that runs alongside Tyburn and further emphasize the leisure use of one space, and the urban reality of transit along the Tadcaster Road with the orbital cycle route.

Furthermore, this juxtaposition ties in with my own observations detailed at the beginning of this chapter, whereby I reduce my embodied experiences of the space and its rhythms — the crows in the tree, my breath in the air — to textual description. The trees, the long grass and the meadow: these reflections are what Shields (1999, p. 60) describes

Figure 2.23. Grass Meadow South of Tyburn

Copyright Matthew Spokes

as 'moments', or 'experiences of detachment from the everyday flow of time, or *durée*' as I consider how the everyday and the urban reality of the space come in to contact and reflect one another. The interplay of the woodland changing with the seasons and the people, roads and fences underscore notable cyclical rhythms – 'long and short times, recurring in recognisable ways, stops, silences, blanks, resumptions and intervals in accordance with regularity' (2004, p. 78). The cyclical interacts with the linear rhythms of the urban, of the 'homogenous parameters' of capitalistic function. It demonstrates the 'antagonistic unity' (2004, p. 76) between spatial elements.

The second use of the space, which corresponds to the urban reality that Lefebvre outlines as well as my own field notes, is for dog walking, a leisure practice that separates out 'useful, productive' time — or the space through which capitalism is able to produce/reproduce value — with time spent in idle pursuits. Again, the leisure pursuit itself is regulated formerly through conceived notions of space, so there are dog waste bins and signs explaining proper behaviour in the woodland (Figure 2.24), but also through the lived practice of the space, that dog walkers walking their dogs expect to see other people walking their dogs. My presence, replete with notebook and AV equipment for taking photos and collecting short films, disrupted this leisure pursuit, and was met with confusion and tacit hostility as noted in the exchange where the '*dog walker eyes me suspiciously as she downs the steps*': even the benches are not meant to be sat on, implying that this space is purely a space of transit.

Figure 2.24. Sign for Dog Walkers

Copyright Matthew Spokes

Having touched on this aspect with regards to dog walkers activities mapping on to connected aspects of urban reality, the third type of use is more directly related, namely the wider networks connecting private space, work space and leisure space. The early morning field notes from Tyburn – collected between 8 a.m. and 9 a.m. – showed the monument site more clearly as a space for transit, with school children cutting through the site to get from the private space of their homes to the work space of school. Similarly, the adjacent cycle routes and the main arterial road also show the relationship between the daily routine of travelling to and from work and the infrastructional network of urban reality in this space.

Additionally, this space is used by people walking to and from the hotels to the south of the site. (The Marriott Hotel is connected directly to the site to the south, and beyond that a Holiday Inn.) In field notes, I have identified that the space is not simply traversed by school children and dog walkers, but a variety of others including parents, a nursery group and, in one slightly surreal episode, a man who approached the gallows site, walked around the forking path in front of it before turning around and walking away. The point is that each of these traversals involves movement through the space that corresponds the functioning of urban reality: the result of this is the development of lived space, of informal paths outside of the remit of planners, created by people engaged in walking, in moving.

Figure 2.25, for example, shows an informal pathway running across the side of the racecourse to the south of Tyburn. The trees flanking this site were littered with burnt debris, empty cans of cider and up-turned crates, suggesting this space is used for other forms of deviant leisure. Figures 2.26 and 2.27 show the main paths that run just south of Tyburn, visible from the site and the primary route of travel for dog walkers and school children across the site: here the informal

Figure 2.25. Path Adjacent to Racecourse

Copyright Matthew Spokes

path is emphasized further by the ways in which the managed space of the woodland has been pared back – the sampling in to the right of the path in Figure 2.26, and the left of the path in Figure 2.27 shows this – facilitating a natural pathway through the trees. In this example, the spaces designed by planners, and those of everyday experience come together.

As Lefebvre outlines (1991, p. 233), social space can be explained and detailed in relation to the combination of stratified codes (paths, routes and fences), the overlapping of objects and forms (people, transport and trees) and intentional signifying processes (maps and historical documents), all of which I have explored over the previous sections of this chapter. However, while it is possible to see the varying elements of the spatial triad manifest in these examples, I would argue that Tyburn itself plays a relatively minimal role, that

Figure 2.26. Path through Woodland Facing North

Copyright Matthew Spokes

the spaces around Tyburn and the uses exemplified so far – while detailing the functionality and uses of different types of space – do little to capture the peculiarities of the area.

An anecdote that problematises spatial understandings of this location may help to elucidate on the concern: following the incident with the man in shorts doubling back on himself, I also saw two men, fully suited and with travel luggage, walking through the woods from south the north. Now whilst it is obviously possible that the two men were walking from the hotels to the south towards the city and/or railway station to the north, this does not change the peculiarity or incongruity of seeing this particular type of person utilising this particular type of space. It is this troubling association that led me to consider a potential way of framing deviant

Figure 2.27. Path through Woodland Facing South

Copyright Matthew Spokes

sites of memorialization like Tyburn through Lefebvre's notion of the 'theatrical'.

2.5. TYBURN AS THEATRICAL SPACE

As Lefebvre argues (1991, p. 38), 'the specific spatial competence and performance of every society member can only be evaluated empirically'. Taking the notion of 'performance' to a slightly different level – and having moved on from my initial unpacking of Lefebvre – I am going to use Tyburn to suggest that while the spatial triad offers us useful insights into the sorts of ways in which space is produced socially around Tyburn, it is less useful in defining exactly what function the Tyburn memorial has. Developing Lefebvre's notion of theatrical space, more commonly associated with artistic framing of activity on the stage (Spokes, 2014), will enable us to more thoroughly reflect and comprehend the shifting associations of Tyburn while reflecting the liminal nature of deviant or criminal spaces of memorialization: from this, it will be possible to posit a scalar approach to understanding heritage in this context.

Tyburn is something of an anomaly: as I have outlined, it is not used in the same functional ways as Little Hob Moor (there is no nature reserve, no allotments echoing the former strip field use), it exists on the fringes of urban reality by being sandwiched between woodland and arterial routes into the city, and although it forms part of the perceived, spatial practices of a variety of people from school children to dog walkers, none of this fully capture the intangible 'essence' of Tyburn as a place. This may be, in part, because of the deviant nature of the locale, and the disjunction between what happened there in the past – something which, while discussed in a relatively anodyne way on the information board, is immortalized elsewhere through symbolic association (Dick Turpin, the pub signs) – and the relative lack of use today. While Little Hob Moor has similar unpleasant associations in a historical sense (the segregation of plague victims), this Othering is symbolized by a connection to the outside world as those with the plague dealt with those who did not have the disease which in turn reinforces the relationship between people. Conversely, Tyburn still represents, in some tacit folk memory, the spectacle of death and the wholesale execution of people deemed criminal which is necessarily played down in a conceived spatial sense by its disconnection with society today: in essence, we are not like those people were.

Rather than speculate further on the interpretive problems of this deviant space, it is worth considering how we might integrate these sorts of space by adapting elements of Lefebvre's corpus to assist us. Lefebvre's codification of space extends beyond the objects, forms, movements and moments previously discussed, to the realm of art – he terms this 'theatrical space'. It is not my intention to suggest that execution is a form of art, but rather that there is value in considering the contemporary nature of spaces of execution, murder and death in relation to artistic tropes, and in that sense we might get closer to understanding the unique nature of historical criminal spatiality.

It is also important to note that although artistic space is delineated from other forms of social practice, it is still predicated on *conceived* and *perceived* spatiality, so I am not throwing the baby out with the conceptual bathwater, but connecting this notion of space with that which I have already unpacked. Theatrical space, Lefebvre suggests, can be *both* of these things:

> *Theatrical space certainly implies a* representation of space – *scenic space - corresponding to a particular* conception *of space (that of the classical drama, say – or the Elizabethan, or the Italian). The* representational space, *mediated yet directly experienced, which infuses the work and the moment, is established as such through the dramatic action itself.* (1991, p. 188)

Theatrical space, in its definitional sense, is interstitial, a space where conventions exist but can be destabilized by 'dramatic action'; again, there may be a tension between each form and this is where dialogue takes place, within a broader assemblage of elements. Theatrical space is typified by an 'interplay between fictitious and real counterparts and its interaction between gazes and mirages in which actor, audience, "characters", text, and author all come together but never become one' (Spokes, 2014). Here Lefebvre is alluding to the shift between the anticipated experience of the physical space (the stage) and the interpretive opportunity which takes place in public but is not itself public; the experience of individual participants in a collective, social activity.

But how might this work with regard to Tyburn, and in what ways does it facilitate a deeper understanding of contested memorial spaces? Let us explore theatrical space by applying some of the conceptual principles Lefebvre offers: this will include 'dramatic action' with regard to 'fictitious and real counterparts'; the stage and the audience; and 'anticipated' experience and 'interpretive' experience.

The dramatic action of the space can be framed in a historical sense both temporally and spatially. In a temporal sense, Tyburn as a site of execution can be considered dramatic in a traditionally theatrical sense; it was a space that attracted tens of thousands of people to watch the execution of criminals. In a spatial sense, the gallows was situated for maximum visibility, as previous discussed, but in its contemporaneous sense the space is now subsumed by residential space, woodland and the various facets of urban reality. So how does dramatic action manifest itself today?

I would argue that as a memorial space, dramatic action now involves the interplay between fictitious and real counterparts. In terms of the 'fictitious', we can see this in relation to the presentation of information at the site which emphasises the grander examples of those executed at the site, such as the notorious highwaymen like 'Dick' Turpin, or the rebels from the Jacobite uprising. I do not mean to say that these people were not executed at the site, that they are fictions, but rather their symbolic function as examples of spectacular

Theatrics (The Tyburn Gallows, York) 69

justice is so great that they marginalise the thousands of other executions that took place over four hundred years. The ways in which memorialization operates today also highlight the juxtaposition between the fictitious and the real. In the case of the former, the 2007 commemoration march for the Jacobite rebels troubles the association between the fictitious and the real. Figures 2.28 and 2.29 show the memorial as a co-opted space where the execution of Scottish rebels is remembered by active engagement with the space and its former function. This is uncharacteristic of the site's day-to-day use and as such problematises the usual daily and urban realities of the space.

In terms of the 'real', there are everyday examples of the use of this space as a memorial and not just as a space where

Figure 2.28. Tributes to the Jacobite Rebels in 2007

© Cranntara 2007

Figure 2.29. Tributes to the Jacobite Rebels in 2007

© Cranntara 2007

people were formerly executed. Of the two benches present on the site, one of them has a plaque attached, memorializing the life of John Thornton who died in 2007 (we can presume he liked sitting at this location, as this is often the way in which bench-memorials are used), so a 'memorial on a memorial' for want of a better description. The Thornton memorial reinforces the changed/changing perception of Tyburn from one associated with execution to one of quiet contemplation, where people can sit and think amongst the mature woodland surrounding the site. Directly opposite Tyburn, down the hill and through the trees, I found another informal memorial that would appear to operate in the same way with a plaque fixed in to a tree on the common land area outside the woodland, dedicated to Jimmy Corr known as 'Pops' (the Thornton and

Figure 2.30. John Thornton Memorial Plaque

Copyright Matthew Spokes

'Pops' memorial can be seen in Figures 2.30 and 2.31). The presence of this memorial so close to the other also suggests that the understanding of this space is one that foregrounds the natural beauty of the land rather than emphasising the former horror that the spectacular examples of execution trade in. These memorial plaques are also related to the more informal examples that have been previously mentioned: the ribbon-bundled sticks I found, and the picture of floors on the noticeboard (Figures 2.1 and 2.3). When combined, they offer an object narrative showing the transformation of space, the parallel lives of the urban reality of networks and paths, the space of contemplation and the historical everyday reality of death.

This arbitrary distinction between fictitious and real is crucial because it demonstrates the multitude of dramatic actions

Figure 2.31. Jimmy Corr Memorial Plaque

Copyright Matthew Spokes

that intersect this location, from the spectacular enactments of Foucauldian bodily punishments to walking the dog. These examples show the everyday reality of memorialization – the presence of the departed as inscribed on the environment on benches and trees – juxtaposed with the spectacular, the Foucauldian framing of bodily punishment and regimes of power; the Scottish memorial re-enactment intentionally invokes and calls upon these bloody associations, to make real what the concrete plaque (Figure 2.1) and woodland obscures. The fact it reinforces the perceived injustice of the past also emphasises the inherent weirdness of the space: a memorial to State-sponsored execution that is now used to commemorate others who enjoyed using the space in its present form as somewhere to sit and think.

Theatrics (The Tyburn Gallows, York)   73

Figure 2.32. Cycle Crossing

Copyright Matthew Spokes

Moving on from 'dramatic action', it is also helpful to consider the physical construction of the Tyburn site as memorial. The first thing that greets the visitor when visiting the site is a particular arrangement of objects in the space, and how they give very little away. There are a series of concrete slabs, flanked to the west by a gap in the white fence that adjoins the site for the length of Tadcaster Road between the Marriott Hotel and the old Huntsman's Cottage. It sits at a road crossing designed specifically for cyclists, as Figure 2.32 shows, and this space is routinely used for the advertising of events happening in and around the area. The slab engraved with 'Tyburn' is small in comparison to the rest of the space, perhaps a third of the size of the benches positioned in front of it, which look away from where the gallows was situated on to the racecourse. I have already highlighted aspects of how this space is performed in a social sense through active and passive memorialization (the Jacobite march, the Thornton plaque), but the physicality of the space can also be considered as a form of staging depending on the perspective of the audience member.

When approached from below, up from the grassland meadow along the gentle gradient of the glacial bank towards Tadcaster Road, the more theatrical aspects of the space are revealed. Figures 2.33 and 2.34 show, first, the interplay of light and shade thrown through the leaves of the surrounding trees, but you can also discern the intentional symmetry of the design. A single row of stairs leading to the Tyburn plinth, flanked on either side by the benches. You climb the

Figure 2.33. Tyburn from Below

Copyright Matthew Spokes

Figure 2.34. Tyburn from Below [shade detail]

Copyright Matthew Spokes

stairs as if ascending to the gallows. There is one way up and one way out. The physical form mirrors the imaginary narrative of an execution, framed by all those associations depicted in the information board on the fringe of the site, here echoing the sort of atmosphere suggested in Stranger and Kempa's (2003) work, introduced in Chapter 1. This is a space of memory, devoid of movement: things around the site may move – the trees, the traffic – but the solid concrete design of the memorial emphasises the finality of it, the rootedness of it within the spaces around it. Yet, as a memorial to something historical, itself the product of multiple representations of space, Tyburn is still difficult to grasp, a memorial to something intangibly unpleasant. The stage is now empty, the 'real' actors departed long ago. Now the audience move across the stage on their way somewhere else. Occasionally people stop for a moment — John Thornton, Jimmy Corr — but then they are gone also.

2.6. CONCLUSION

What this assemblage of elements means is that Tyburn never fully coalesces as a comprehensible space. It is liminal. Characters, text and authors come together but only ever in partial arrangements, a robust example of the interrelations between anticipated experience and interpretive opportunity that Lefebvre (1991) discusses.

In this chapter, I have used the case study of the deviant space of Tyburn to think through some of the ways in which Lefebvre's spatial triad can be used to explore contentious locations as produced socially. In doing so, I identified some less-than-useful aspects of this approach, namely that while the troika of conceived, lived and perceived space enables the researcher to unpack and outline the spaces interconnected with Tyburn, they do not help in the conceptual outlining of the liminality of these extraordinary spaces in a spatio-temporal sense. Drawing on Lefebvre's concept of the theatrical allowed me to foreground the more illusory aspects of memorialization, memory and physicality, and questions the associations that develop in relation to the past and contemporary uses of criminal space. I should stress that this has been entirely experimental, and is not offered as a solid blueprint for further action — Lefebvre routinely states that the construction of rigid boundaries of analysis restricts spatial understanding and engagement (2005) — but rather a series of interjections and suggestions that, where deviant space is involved, a critical vocabulary and set of conceptual tools is needed that develops the existing spatial theory towards an appreciation of this type of diversity: the memorial to State-sponsored murder as a lived artefact (see Figure 2.35).

Figure 2.35. Tyburn Reverse Angle

Copyright Matthew Spokes

NOTES

1. For those interested, the first execution at the Castle did not take place for almost a year after Tyburn was closed. James Roberts was the first man executed on the new gallows: he was convicted of stealing 19 sheep, and was hanged alongside William's Baker and Jackson on the 26 August 1802. Despite being decommissioned, the gallows continued to stand at the site until 1812 when it was eventually removed (Knipe, 1867).

2. So named because it could hang three people at once.

3. This can be seen in promotional material for a variety of ghost walks across the city (somewhere in the region of 10 at last count, the slightly-more-recent addition of 'murder tours', the Necrobus service – a guided tour bus route that asks us to 'behold the gruesome past' and the long-standing York Dungeons franchise.

CHAPTER 3

CONSUMPTION (NUMBER 25 CROMWELL STREET, GLOUCESTER)

Lefebvre titled his book, *The Production of Space* (1991), and the contested and interrelated ways in which space is produced has so far been explored at the Tyburn site in York. This chapter develops the previous, exploring what happens when the production of space is positioned in opposition to its consumption.

> *In extreme cases, more drastic action may be required, such as in the case of 25 Cromwell Street, Gloucester, the home of Frederick and Rosemary West and the site of multiple murders by the couple. In 1996, following their trial and imprisonment, the house was demolished and the site transformed into a pathway to prevent it becoming a ghoulish shrine.*
> *(Sharpley, 2009, p. 9)*

Contrary to the previous chapter, I have never been to Cromwell Street and this is an analysis of a space through documentary research instead. Number 25 Cromwell Street (henceforth referred to as Number 25) was demolished in 1996 and in its place now stands a memorial walkway – an effort by Gloucester Council to expunge the site from memory saw the complete destruction and redistribution, even of the rubble of the building. Now, the garden under which several of the Wests' victims were buried is extended into a memorial-space-cum-pedestrian pathway as the Victorian semi-detached, along with the empty house next door, has been removed from the end of a row of remaining terraces. Now the space consists of a sweeping pathway that jarringly changes colour from the old tarmac to the new, as number 21 to the left – and the Seventh Day Adventist Church to the right – give way to this conspicuous gap in the urban landscape. This recent addition of absence to Cromwell Street, a scar in an otherwise neat row of houses, exposes some hidden intimate past by laying bare the guts of this gruesome burial site. Tarmac stops and block paving starts as this memorial becomes an understated walkway, blocked off from traffic by seven black bollards on the front facing end. Progressing from Cromwell Street, the walkway leads you through into an existing alley that connects to St Michael's Square, a quadrant of houses around a public car park.

This decision to destroy Number 25 was part of a complex negotiation of heritage that local councils and communities experience when wanting to memorialise victims of infamous death and violence, without enshrining the spaces for souvenir-hunters or dark tourists. The conflicting agendas can be separated into three parts; the desire to memorialize dead victims; the will to remove the difficult heritage of violence despite extensive media coverage; and the need for a usable and safe public place. These map onto Lefebvre's spatial triad, and will be analysed through spatial practice (media coverage); representations of space (that I will be terming anti-memorialization) and representational space (dark tourism). This chapter furthers debates in the politics of the memorialization of death and atrocity by contributing an analysis of Number 25 – the former home and current memorial of notorious British serial murderers Fred and Rose West, and the death of their victims, respectively. It follows on from the previous chapter in embracing Henri Lefebvre's spatial triad as a central lens of analysis – and uses the framework laid down for incorporating his notion of 'theatrical space' as an addition. Building on this framework from the previous chapter, theatrical space will be further legitimised as useful for not only the multifarious contexts of problematic deviant memorializations, but as particularly useful for those cases with modern, infamous celebrity connections and excessive media coverage.

My approach is to use available imagery, local council documentation and past and present media coverage to perform a media/documentary analysis of this space of death and pain. I will argue that theatrical space, explained in the previous chapter, is particularly useful when unpacking infamous or celebrity memorials that have enjoyed extensive media coverage. After putting into practice this framework from the previous chapter, I will make the additional contribution of introducing Lefebvre's (1991) concept of contradictory space as a way to understand the conflicting nodes of spatial production in an infamous, criminal-celebrity, memorial setting. It will be argued that, out of the contradictory performances of death through media coverage against the lack of death through local governmental policy comes the lived space that is defined by the contested consumption of death.

3.1. SOME CONTEXT

Perhaps the words of journalist Euan Ferguson from 2004, some 10 years after the atrocity, can give the reader a feeling of the space at hand:

> *Gloucester shouts paradoxically loudly, to me, this day, about the one thing it never mentions, will never mention, hopes against hope would simply be gone forever [...]. Walk past the ruins, down Eastgate, cut down the side of Sloane's bar, down the back of Argos and the Mecca Bingo. Wrap your coat a little tighter as you cross the Hampden Way car park and skirt the Shopmobility stand, where 35 tattered electric buggies huddle against a feral wind, and you are, suddenly, in Cromwell Street. Right there [...], there is nothing. The absence yells. There is, instead, a little Tarmac walkway, through to an alley and another car park. The walkway has 16 cast-iron black bollards, unappealing pyracantha bushes down the sides, a little blue sign warning against drinking in public, and a couple of battered empty cans of Stella. (Guardian Online, 2004)*

The absence of the house of Fred and Rose West is a common sense — yet totally conspicuous attempt at removing memory from the physical space that it occupies. Of course, there was not always nothingness here. A decision had to be taken by the Council, after consulting the local residents, to remove the house:

> *Much of Gloucester's anger is directed at this forsaken, crumbling house. The locals want something done about it. Property prices in Cromwell Street have plunged. Ted Wynn, of the*

> *Gloucester estate agents ME Wynn & Co, says the entire street has been afflicted, with a six-bedroom house that should have sold for pounds 60,000 now on the market for little more than half that amount. In weeks gone by, police and journalists have often outnumbered residents. And, worst of all, ghoulish, camera-wielding sight-seers have started to come and gawp. [...] Suggestions for alternative uses so far include a shrine or memorial garden for the victims or a hostel for vulnerable young people.*
> *(Independent Online, 1995)*

This question of what can be done to temper ghoulish sight-seers while maintaining a level of tasteful memorialisation is one that can be approached through Lefebvre's notion of contradictory space. The *Daily Mail* has made this enquiry before now as well: 'what should be done with the sordid sites of serial killer's homes' (Mail Online, 2012)? Featuring the American killer Jeffrey Dahmer's childhood home and site of first victim, they detail his crimes and question whether selling these houses at cut down rates (generally around 25% less) to be used again as family homes is entirely appropriate (ibid.). No less than eight examples from recent history in this single article show the scale of the problem of memorialisation of places of death and violent crime, of preservation or of destruction. According to the *Daily Mail*, some of these heritage sites can become thriving businesses. For example, the Lizzie Borden Bed and Breakfast Museum (Lizzie-Borden.com, n.d.) offers visitors an 'authentic' experience of the Massachusetts murders in Borden's house, with a hotel backdrop.

But there has been a sustained pushback by local councils against this trend, most notably in the cases of the (2002) murders by Ian Huntley of Holly Wells and Jessica Chapman in Soham, and of the infamous British serial killers, Fred and

Rose West. Their respective places of residence, in both Soham and Gloucester, have been the subject of controversy regarding their post-crime preservation in the sense that Sharon Macdonald (1998) refers to as the 'politics of display' and of preservation. It remains unclear to what extent these sites are memorials, public spaces or dark tourist sites, but it is evident that juggling these three interlinked positions has been a problem for local councils and communities. This also amplifies questions raised in Chapter 2 of the nature of space more generally, and the degree to which that is tied to its sustained use in a social and relational sense. To foster memory through memorial for the victims, while simultaneously expunging the memory and association with death and notoriety and the dark tourism (Stone, 2009), or even the under-researched area of 'murderabilia' (Denham, 2016), that comes with it has proven a difficult negotiation.

This chapter considers Fred and Rose West and their Cromwell Street home. After the exposure of their murders, there was an extensive media debate surrounding the future of this space ending with the demolition of Number 25 in mid-October 1996. Gloucester City Council took an aggressive approach to dealing with this heritage site: reportedly melting down the fittings, burning the timbers, crushing the bricks and using them to fill 'undisclosed parts of the council waste tip' (Independent Archives Online, 1996). During the demolition, mounted police patrolled the street attempting to stop 'ghoulish souvenir-hunters plundering the house and garden' (ibid.). Gloucester Council saw this approach of total destruction as appropriate due to the 'sensitive nature' of the space (ibid.), but that has not stopped dark tourists from making the pilgrimage. The *Independent* also reported that a survey by Robertson Bell Associates was to be carried out as a 'public consultation exercise' regarding the future of the space after demolition – the survey would take into account opinions of victims' relatives and local residents (ibid.). The outcome was unfortunately never published, although it resulted in the preservation of the site as a shrub-lined public walkway and memorial for the victims. This quote from *BBC News* provides a footing for analysis:

> *The decision to get rid of all physical traces of the house was presented at the time as a way of expunging the sense of evil linked to the place – and on the assumption that no one would want to live in a place with so many grim associations. (BBC News, 2004)*

Statements by the media imply a symbolic importance of the bricks and mortar first, and second the space in which they stood, to the crimes of Fred and Rose and the deaths of their victims. They also make the self-confessed assumption that nobody would want to live in such a space despite counter evidence that violent criminal houses tend to be sold into homes and businesses rapidly, or make popular (albeit unsavoury) tourist attractions.

According to Sharon Macdonald, buildings are 'one of the most pronounced forms of heritage' (2009, p. 25) with strong symbolic association – which goes some way to explaining why we are determined to rid ourselves of ones with negative or 'difficult' histories. This is in part due to their ability to convey meanings over time and the immense power over memory that these physical structures possess. They are likely, writes Macdonald, to perpetuate continuities in identity over time. The tendency to demolish violent structural histories in this context is likely due to their ability to 'give testimony', to provide a reference point against which criminal memory is anchored. While council and media approaches to difficult heritage in this case study are public knowledge, the spatial dynamics of this approach to memorialization have gone unanalysed, that is, the systematic and total destruction of structures with negative symbolic power in an effort to stem the negative heritages that come with death, while simultaneously honouring the victims. Let us finish this section with some more from Ferguson's ethnography:

> *Not a plaque, not a hint, let alone a memorial garden. A bit of concrete, and lousy green shrubs, and wet litter, and a nasty little wind sighing more loudly through the walkway as darkness falls. 'Not a very nice site, no,' comes the quiet agreement from the church's pastor, Stefan Burton-Schnüll, as I gaze around at the trees growing crisp-bags and the mud morphing into dog-shit; 'but it was decided not to commemorate it in any way, out of respect for the victims.' Rose Wests' lawyer, Leo Goatley, concurs. There is, he says, 'something of an eerie silence about the footpath'. (Guardian Online, 2004)*

Ferguson alludes to some aspects of Lefebvrian spatiality already introduced. He points to the lack of spectacle and of theatre, describing the place as uniquely drab for somewhere the focus of so much media outcry. Then there is a seemingly contradictory quote from the church pastor highlighting the contradictory space — aren't memorials usually a sign of respect for victims? It is interesting to further research in difficult heritage and dark tourism by investigating the spatial dynamics of this anti-memorial. The coming sections will consider the absence of physical reminders of death through Lefebvre's spatial triad[1] and the notion of theatrical space — before suggesting some of the facets of Lefebvre's 'contradictory space' as useful for decoding the contradicting demands of memorial and souvenir in cases of infamous death.

3.2. NUMBER 25 AS PERCEIVED SPACE

Number 25, like Tyburn in the previous chapter, also contains elements of these spatial engagements of use, historical association and representation. Spatial practice is how space is used – the outcome of the individual's choices and decisions inside of space. The Cromwell Street walkway is a perceived space in its existence as a connection between nodes of urban life in the first instance, and in the second, in its existence as a site of intense media coverage. It is a perceived space for those who pass through it as part of the ordinary flows of urban life, but also as a space where the symbolism of death has been layered by the media as such to encourage the consumption of death – interpreted as what Lefebvre (1991) refers to as daily reality and urban reality, respectively.

In the first instance, then, the walkway is a pass-through between Cromwell Street and St Michael's Square. It is used by passers-by who, for over a decade now, have been utilising this fresh cut-through as they do their daily reality inside of an urban reality that has been reshaped by death; this has altered the flow of pedestrian traffic, repositioning the church onto a corner and bringing the car park temporally closer to Gloucester Park to the south, the Royal Hospital to the north, and the rest of the Victorian housing that makes up eastern Gloucester. It has altered the rhythmic flow of urban life that Lefebvre has argued constitutes the social – its 'recognisable ways, stops, silences, blanks, resumptions and intervals' (2004, p. 78) have been amended by this memorial.

It connects private and public spaces together, the car park with the housing estate, and the supermarket with western Gloucester. By contrast, the spatial practice of Tyburn included an impromptu, informal network of pathways that problematised the established function of urban reality, the flows of people through the Cromwell Street Walkway are not open to interpretation or improvement. They are instead corralled by the local authority through this new connection between the established nodes of the city. For the local authority, the Cromwell Street Walkway should fulfil the spatial practice of a walkway and nothing more.

In the second instance, the walkway is a perceived space through its media sensationalisation as a place of death and suffering. The Wests' have been the subject of numerous films, have been covered in television programmes and have been the subject of several books (for example, Woodrow, 2012; Jarrold, 2011; Anderson, 2014). They have been cemented by the news media as infamous popular cultural icons of death and violence. This media exposure will have altered the perception of the Cromwell Street space by attaching symbolic representational association with death. However, I will avoid going into any more detail here, as the results of this will be touched upon under the subheading representational space and will be further unpacked as part of theatrical space towards the end.

3.3. NUMBER 25 AS CONCEIVED SPACE

The Cromwell Street memorial, as a conceived space, is antagonistic to being used, or at the very least, selectively obstructive as a memorial space. By contrast, spatial practice has consisted of a network of pedestrian movements and excessive media symbolism of death and criminality, the space conceived by the local authority is what I will refer to as 'anti-memorial'. Lefebvre (1991, p. 222) reminds us that 'conceived space is a place for the practices of social and political power; in essence, it is these spaces that are designed to manipulate those who exist in them' — the planners and legislators of the Cromwell Street Walkway have achieved this through the means of destruction; understatement; and lack of facility. In a hunt to quash dark tourism, planners have excavated the memory of death from the urban landscape along with the bodies themselves.

In terms of this destruction, the decision by the Gloucester Council to dismantle and extinguish from memory the house and property of the infamous serial killers is the one most obviously interpreted as the enactment of representations of space by political structures. We can turn to the Gloucester Police for an insight into the before and after:

> *25 Cromwell Street was a semi-detached three-storey house which adjoined a void property, number 23 Cromwell Street. On the northern side of the property was a Seventh Day Adventist Church. (Police Document, p. 27)*

Police were left with a semi-detached house where multiple people were murdered, alongside its abandoned counterpart. Faced with the will to shape this landscape away from death, murder and dark tourism, the process of anti-memorial was begun:

> *All the effects from 25 Cromwell Street which were taken into police possession during the search were recorded systematically onto an exhibits computer package. This resulted in the recording of over 1300 items, which included every type of household effect that would normally be found in any family home [...] some items were returned to members of the family whilst a large volume of household effects were destroyed by mutual agreement in controlled conditions, thus preventing souvenir hunters from acquiring any items then or in the future. (Police Document, p. 43)*

Ideologically, it is visible in today's walkway that those decision makers wanted the memory of death to be destroyed on Cromwell Street. Following the destruction of personal effects as listed by the Police Department in deterrence of dark tourism came the demolition of the houses and the destruction of bricks and rubble in a similar fashion.

Nations have a tendency to attempt disappearing acts on their difficult heritage architecture. From the demolition of Armenian churches in Turkey, to the Chinese removal of Tibetan Buddhist monasteries (Macdonald, 2009), history is rife with examples of nations attempting to remove the power of storytelling from controversial spaces (ibid.). The same patterns of removal were witnessed in Nuremberg (ibid.) and can be seen in gender (Cote, 2009) heritage also. This tendency towards removal is not unique to governments, and is in no way unique to national or 'macro' sites of difficult heritage despite a research focus on these areas. Architecturally bound memories, patterns of preservation and destruction and political manipulations of heritage are extremely visible in the conceived space of local difficult heritage in the context of violent death. In Cromwell Street, after destruction, all that was left was a blank plot of land, ready for a fresh segment of the urban landscape to be conceived by the local authority.

In 2017, we are left with the walkway that Ferguson had described to us over a decade ago. It has worn in, now, with the seedlings that once flanked the sides grown up into bushes that overlap the grass edging. The Council has provided an extensive pattern of black traffic-limiting bollards to corral pedestrians through the walkway – these are elements of conceived space that interfere with readjusted rhythms. The bollards stop cars from entering or exiting the walkway, but they also dictate a long line through the middle that seems to serve no purpose other than as a signifier of two lanes of traffic, hurrying passers-by through and towards their destinations. Tarmac gives way to block paving as the space for cars becomes a space for people, but these bollards are as unwelcoming for people as the harshness of the roadways. This is not a place that invites people to come and stay, to rest and think, to mourn the dead or celebrate the killers.

Signage acknowledges the Square through the walkway, or the park if you are emerging from the other side, but does not commemorate the presence of death or deviance here. Two tall, black street lamps sit along the left, further abstracting a sense of deviance that comes with alleyways that are left dark and offering a literal affront to 'dark tourism' that the council has so staunchly fought. Benches, resting places or monuments that would usually be associated with memorialization are absent. Tradition gives way in Cromwell Street to thorny bushes with orange berries that invite the urban pedestrian to do nothing more than pass through on their way to a destination away from here.

The topic of forgetting, while going hand in hand with social memory, is not something that we always consider when researching death – and Lefebvre's acknowledgement of the political overlays on urban space gives us a good grounding to think about forgetting and memorial. '[F]orgetting is a difficult and thorny matter: One can remember and remember to remember, and one can also develop techniques to help one remember, but a technique to forget becomes immediately paradoxical' (Esposito, 2008, p. 181). It is paradoxical in that to think about forgetting is to immediately remember – the problem of reflexivity – but in an urban landscape, stark nothingness can be equally jarring.

Elsewhere (Denham, 2016) I have written about the selectivity of cultural memory associated with deviance, and how the romantic or charismatic elements of infamous acts of deviance or death are selectively privileged in the material afterlife of criminality. I was writing about the phenomena of 'murderabilia' — morbid memorabilia and collectables associated with violent crimes — but the same can be true when tales of death transition into spaces as well as objects. I argued (p. 231), that through the process of materialisation and commodification, some of the more visceral aspects of death were 'selectively forgotten', making way for infamous narrative afterlives to develop. The anti-memorial is the politicised act of selective remembrance. The council, in anti-memorialization, can be seen as manipulating the selectivity of collective cultural memory.

3.4. NUMBER 25 AS LIVED SPACE

For Lefebvre, lived space is made up of the signs and symbols that shape people's actual experience of a space. The individual meaning of this space, then, or the person's 'everyday life' in space is highly contested due to the conflicting forces of media coverage of death, and the local council's attempts to remove death from the landscape. At this point, we can consider the use of this urban space as influenced by the symbolic perceived space of media coverage, as well as the conceived space of anti-memorial — as a dark tourist attraction.

Rhythms of urban life are further altered in its lived space as a dark tourist site as the space has become a tourist destination in and of itself. As recently as February 2017, British tabloid newspaper the *Sun* reports that 'thousands of people [are] visiting the side of Fred and Rose Wests' house in [a] creepy craze where people flock to scenes of murders and disasters' (Sun Online, 2017). While the empirical accuracy of these claims is questionable, it is not an exaggeration that dark tourists have caused headaches for those maintaining infamous, gruesome sites of death and suffering.

The way in which the space is used in the very tangible sense of market demand seems to be as a space for the ghoulish souvenir hunters and dark tourists. They have made this place a cornerstone of criminal-celebrity after immeasurable hours of media coverage that have carved out, alongside the Moors Murderers Myra Hindley and Ian Brady, a niche of notoriety for the Wests' in contemporary British culture.

> *Heritage theorists note that 'dark' places are especially marketable if they were notorious, if the perpetrators of death or pain were especially cruel [...] or if those who suffered were famous or especially sympathetic victims. (Tunbridge and Ashworth, 1996, pp. 104–105)*

These qualities of criminal celebrity go hand in hand with the groundwork of dark tourism. Tunbridge and Ashworth remind us that those characters celebrated through tourism need be notorious, cruel, with particularly sympathetic victims – qualities that the Wests' have in bundles after extensive media coverage of the gruesome murders of minors. It was inevitable, then, that the lived space of Number 25 would fall to this well-established phenomenon of death tourism as visitors interpret the site through the mediatised symbolic overlay of death, rather than any physical presence of death itself. Seaton (1996) argues that long before tourism for the purpose of leisure, death has been a catalyst of travel, frequently through religious pilgrimage. Smith continues arguing that war tourism is likely the single largest category in the world (1998). For Seaton and Smith, dark tourism is age old, a notion that is confirmed when considering Roman gladiatorial games and sites of public execution (Stone and Sharpley, 2008).

Among the items destroyed by the Gloucester Council to temper this spatial practice was the signage – '25 Cromwell St' – written in white slanted italics inside of a black metal frame. This, among other signifiers of authentic criminality that are directly recognisable as West murderabilia, would have been the most desirable objects for tourists and collectors. Without these signifiers, the tourists still flock to Cromwell Street, but are greeted with an impotent experience of death subdued from the urban landscape. The removal and destruction of these signifiers can be seen as acts of conceived space, attempts to shape remembrance and the historical ideology of death in Gloucester by legislators.

Lennon and Foley suggest that 'the immediacy of the tragedy and the relative "closeness" [are why] Cromwell Street attracted many visitors to the UK's most recent site of multiple murder' (2006, p. 160) – yet there is no trace of death here on the walkway, visitors are not close to any remnants of death whatsoever. Even now, decades later and after the immediacy has faded, tourists still visit. The *Daily Mirror* has summed up this contradiction:

> *It may have been demolished 20 years ago – after the remains of nine young women were found buried beneath the property – but that doesn't stop people being intrigued. The infamous site in Cromwell Street was actually knocked down and replaced by an alleyway – making it easy for people to inspect. (Mirror Online, 2017)*

This media discourse reminds us that nothingness has not stopped dark tourism in this space, and suggests that if anything, the lack of a house has allowed visitors to get even closer to the murder scene. If a house was still present, the garden where victims were buried – or the space over the basement where murders took place — would be out of bounds. This is the observation that, in the sense of the perceived space of the walkway, visitors are allowed to get temporally closer to death than before. In terms of the lived space, they are symbolically closer to the site of death despite markings and remnants long since destroyed. The *Mirror* even interviewed some tourists themselves about the symbolic (representational) allure of the Cromwell Street walkway, quoting one as saying:

> *By the time I'd moved here, the house had been demolished so there wasn't anything actually to see. But just the curiosity of coming here, seeing where everything took place, the fact this was a normal street and these were horrific crimes committed by somebody who is well known in the area, was just fascinating to me. (Dark Tourist cited in Mirror Online, 2017)*

In pointing out that there was not anything to actually see, the tourist is referring to the bricks and mortar remnants of the Cromwell Street property over the space that it occupies — but he is still able to see where everything took place. The space conceived by the council, and all of the work done to remove death from memory at Cromwell Street, does not stop death from symbolically occupying the blank area left behind. This is 'lived space', the space made up from signs, symbols and symbolic association.

He then points out that this is just a 'normal' street, but that the Wests' wellknownness — earned through media exposure — rendered the space symbolically more interesting. Indeed, it is true that many spaces where a similar number of people have lost their lives are not reified or enshrined with the same aura of death. The Wests' former residence is a popular site of tourist consumption because of the symbolic meaning, conjured by the media, which constitute this representational space.

3.5. THEATRICAL SPACE OR WATCHED SPACE?

Emma Willis (2014) has written of the theatricality of death in public spaces and of dark tourism as well. 'Both theatre and dark tourism are haunted by absence and, each in their own manner, traffic in substitutes that attempt to make such absence present, to make it *felt*' (2014, p. 17, original emphasis). Cromwell Street is certainly haunted by absence, but this is absence by design with substitutes trafficked to further deplete any indicators of the history that once stood between the church and Number 21. 'Tourist attractions', Willis writes, 'often seek to engage visitors through an attention to elements such as staging' (ibid., p. 30). But these are the theatrics of making death *felt* as part of space – it seems convoluted to write of the theatrics of absence as opposed to theatrics as an affront to absence.

We highlighted in the previous chapter that Lefebvre's theatrical space is interspatial – he describes it himself as an 'interplay between fictitious and real counterparts and its interaction between gazes and mirages in which actor, audience, "characters", text, and author all come together but never become one' (1991, p. 188). It is a space in which representations of space (conceived) interact with and overlay representational space (lived) as a sort of performance, in this case, of nothingness. This performative element makes it particularly useful when we begin to apply his spatial dynamics to infamous cases that have been subjected to intense media coverage.

The physical space of the Cromwell Street Walkway is juxtaposed against the opportunity for interpretation or experience of individual participants in a collective, social activity. We have discussed how this performance of interpretation is influenced by representations of space as a local council policy of anti-memorialization. But considering this interaction as performative allows us to further think about representations of space in the opposite sense – as the extensive and sustained media coverage of deviance. On the one hand, Gloucester Council's conception of Number 25 is that of nothingness. On the other, the mainstream media's conception of the street is of unabated deviance and death.

Earlier I wrote that 'stark nothingness was jarring' and acted against the local authority's attempts to expunge memory through conceived space – but the theatrics developed from endless media coverage of this infamous case have laid the groundwork for considering the space as urban performance. As we already know, theatrical space is predicated on *conceived* (anti-memorial) and *perceived* (dark tourism) notions of space. Following this, and by considering how the contradictory performance of death (media) and anti-memorial (council) work theatrically, we can again explore our case study by applying some of the conceptual principles Lefebvre offers associated with theatrical space: these were 'dramatic action' with regard to 'fictitious and real counterparts'; the stage and the audience; and anticipated and interpretive experiences.

Number 25 can be considered as dramatic, temporally, in that it played host to some of the most notorious atrocities and deaths in British history. Spatially, though, there is nothing. The contemporary space of the Cromwell Street Walkway has left no hint or trace of death on the landscape whatsoever. There are no formal memorial plaques, as in Tyburn, to symbolically refer back to death as part of a performance of death occupying space. Nor is there the visible differentiation previously mentioned between the fictitious and the real. In Tyburn, an acknowledgement of Richard 'Dick' Turpin was enshrined as part of the theatrical production of death in space. The fictitious or mediated narratives of death are the only ones still present at the Cromwell Street. The dramatic action of the walkway, originally referred to by Lefebvre in a traditional sense as theatre, has become inescapably mediated – Number 25 is only associated with death when literally used as the theatrical stage for media coverage of the Wests.

If the Tyburn memorial gives little away as the visitor approaches, the conceived space of the Cromwell Street Walkway is a performance of routine, urban, lived space and of nothingness when it comes to death. The bollards that corral pedestrians through the unmarked walkway set the stage for the collective forgetting of death in the urban landscape. In terms of the audience, understanding this walkway as a form of performance becomes more complicated. The stage is very empty, both as a space of death and of representations of death, but the audience still move across it as both viewers of mainstream media and as those still doing daily reality inside of urban reality.

Theatrical space, in this context, can be interpreted as the *watched space* rather than in its more literal sense of the performance of death. 'Audience' as media viewers are conditioned to see it as a space hugely symbolic of death – just the mere mention of *Cromwell Street* puts the public in mind of murder, as well as the infamous image of this row of three-storey Gloucester terraces. 'The relevance of the media for individual and social forms of memory is widely acknowledged by representatives of memory studies' (Zierold, 2008, p. 399) – it is impossible to ignore this aspect of spatial consumption as part of the theatrical audience. The audience as dark tourists do the same, they interpret the walkway as temporally connected to death and atrocity despite the stage, and the slate, having been wiped clean – the theatrics of death are inescapable for this reason of audience interpretation.

Lefebvre (1991) writes of anticipated and interpretive experiences. The local authority has used conceived space to produce an empty stage devoid of references to death. In Lefebvre's terms, this can be understood as the anticipated experience of space. But the interpretive experience conjured by those who consume the space – as opposed to those who live it, embeds the theatrics of death in Cromwell Street.

So we have considered perceived space (dark tourism) and conceived space (anti-memorial) through theatre and positioned them in opposition to one another – what is left from Lefebvre's triad is this third element of lived space – the space that is actually interpreted and experienced by people. Theatrically, Lefebvre describes this last piece thusly: 'the lived space, mediated yet directly experienced, which infused the work and the moment, is established as such through dramatic action itself' (1991, p. 188). In other words, the lived space is the space of performative experience – the corner of the triad where the other two contradictory elements of Cromwell Street collide.

3.6. THEATRICAL SPACE AS CONTRADICTORY SPACE

At this point, we are still left with a highly contested and contradictory lived space. The urban space itself is devoid of references to death, but the space that we consume through media and tourism is still very much symbolic of a ghoulish past – here is where I shall argue that these contested and multifarious agendas can be best understood as part of Lefebvre's contradictory space, that can account for these contradictions between the space that is physically lived, and that that is lived through media and symbolic performance.

It was highlighted in the previous chapter that the corners of Lefebvre's triangular theory do not represent exclusive, distinguishable values. In part, Lefebvre juggles these overlaps with an acknowledgement of what he calls 'contradictory space'. He writes: 'dialectical thinking has been bound up with time: contradictions voice or express the forces and the relationships between forces that clash within a history' (Lefebvre, 1991, p. 292). For Lefebvre, no space is without contradiction – relationships are that of 'inclusion and exclusion, conjunction and disjunction' (p. 293) in that to frame a space towards one discourse, say, the conceived space of the anti-memorial, is to place it in opposition to the alternative agenda.

What can be seen in memorials of infamous death is a concentrated microcosm of Lefebvre's contradictory space – the three corners of the triad pushing against each other as 'historical, physical, linguistic' (p. 292) 'traits' are in friction in these highly contested, media scrutinised, locally contingent, governmentally politicised spaces. The space in question is not a memorial, nor a tourist attraction, or a walkway, but a set of experiences that cannot be separated from the context of their experience. It depends then on how the space is used, or *lived* – this illusive and interpretive third piece of the triad. Lefebvre refers to this personal interaction with space as the transition a person should make from the 'space of its body to its body in space' (p. 294) – but the central message is that space is not a means for classification, or a space to be classified in, but an interaction between the person and the nodes of the spatial triad. Contradictory space, then, is the acknowledgement of these conflicting, and sometimes contested, values and experiences of place.

The contest between dark tourists, on the one hand, and the local community and Council, on the other, is highly visible in these terms. Different people have different involvements and relationships with space, but it is not enough to chalk these inconsistent practices up to personal experience. The perceived space of dark tourism and the conceived space of anti-memorial are engaged in a simultaneous effort to remove the other in a truly contested, contradictory way – relationships of 'inclusion and exclusion', in sites of infamous death and dark tourism, play out in opposition to each other, juxtaposed against both parties who also use the lived space of the walkway with or without acknowledgement of this contest.

The premise for the *Sun*'s (2017) aforementioned claim about the popularity of dark tourism at the Wests' house comes from a recent documentary by Chris Lloyd (2017) called *Dark Tourism*. In the trailer, the documentary maker is standing holding a camera on a tripod, snapping images of the scene. A passer-by, presumably a local resident, disappears into a gravel driveway while engaging the cameraman in conversation. 'Are you taking pictures of where the serial killer used to live?' After receiving no answer, he offers his opinion – 'well you're a bit sick if you are'.

Difficult heritage research has touched upon this role of local residents in suppressing memories attached to places. For example, Macdonald (2009, p. 53) tells an account of an Austrian conference delegate who was refused directions to the Nuremberg site of the Nazi rally grounds by a hotel receptionist in the 1970s. The Cromwell Street is a place that is truly contradictory in public interest and fascination as positioned against the political overlay of absence and purging of memory. This is something that death studies have acknowledged before, albeit in different terms.

Philip Stone (2009), seminal dark tourism researcher, has referred to the way that societies cope with death as part of an 'absent-present paradox' in acknowledgement that, in death-spaces, we are simultaneously engaged in taming or hiding away death, while recognising and respecting its presence through memorial. While Stone is writing about the absent-death thesis (ideas that death is being negotiated increasingly privately in a more personal sense), this is nonetheless relevant to the Cromwell Street. He goes on to argue that dark tourism can be understood as 'making absent death present' in the public consciousness (2009, p. 36), and this is true for the perceived space of death in Gloucester. But the conceived space of the walkway serves a contradictory purpose and in that sense is quite the opposite, it is designed to make the presence of death in the public consciousness as absent as possible. So what does this mean for the audience, the theatrically lived space, which has to juggle these two contradictory goals?

3.7. THE SPACE OF CONSUMPTION

One of Lefebvre's central contradictions in space is that of the 'space of consumption, which coincides with the historical locations of capital accumulation, with the space of production, and with the space that is produced' (1991, p. 352). Lefebvre is referring directly to the interests of business and of capital on the production of space — the interests of consumption alter and conflict with the space that is produced.

Similar language has been used in the study of infamousness in a different way. In his essay on the famous and infamous 'mass idols' of contemporary popular culture, Leo Lowenthal (1961) used comparable terms to describe the changing nature of celebrated figures. From idols of production, he argues, to idols of consumption. Those celebrated in the past were the producers of society — doctors or politicians. Those celebrated now are the consumers of society — actors, 'talentless' celebrities — though more recent research into fandom (Penfold-Mounce, 2010) shows we can add criminal celebrities to that list.

It seems that production, in terms of infamous memorial spaces, can be understood as the stage, this is the conceived space of the anti-memorial and the perceived space of mediated death creating a contradictory, contested performance. What is left over is the lived space — the symbolic space experienced by the audience in this performance. This is the space that can be understood as the space of consumption as dark tourism persists through the combination of signs and symbols that have attached themselves to the Cromwell Street Walkway, despite there being no physical trace of death left behind. In asking: why do dark tourists still seek out a space with no physical remnants of death? We can see that visitors are consuming the signs and symbols of death that have been attached to the place through popular media coverage in the lived, representational space.

The walkway is a literal space of production in a number of senses. It represents the production of social memory (or in this case, forgetting). It is the conceived space of a walkway that connects two parts of Gloucester. Through that walkway, it also produces and alters flows of daily life inside of urban space. However, this is contradicted by the ways in which it is also a space of consumption; it is a space of consumption in the very literal sense of those who consume death through dark tourism on the site — but also in terms of consumption through the excessive news media coverage and popular cultural attention that the house and subsequent walkway have been subject to. More abstractly, serial murder itself has been likened to extreme and excessive consumer capitalism (Jarvis, 2007) in its rhythmic and cyclical processes of selecting an object of desire, using it up, and then starting over again. In the Cromwell Street Walkway, dark tourists are consuming symbolic media narratives of death in place of the physical remnants of death themselves.

3.8. CONCLUSION

What I am arguing is not against Lefebvre's spatial triad, or the concepts of theatrical space that we developed previously. Rather, I am suggesting that spatial practices of the media coverage of Cromwell Street contradict and rub against the conceived space of the anti-memorial — and that the result of this, the experience of the audience in a theatrical sense, can be better understood as the space of consumption as part of lived space. The space experienced by pedestrians, residents and dark tourists is as a result of the contradictory, theatrical performances of local government and national media. The result is a space that is lived through consumption — both literally consumed in terms of dark tourism, and symbolically in terms of media attention.

It is worth noting at this end point that Lefebvre is critical of attempts to unpick these contradictions, despite providing us with a framework through which to do so. We are asked, as critics, to be aware of 'both a false consciousness of abstract space and an objective falseness of space itself' (1991, p. 298). In fact, Lefebvre is better known for putting things together rather than taking them apart. In *Rhythmanalysis*, he urges that we, as researchers of social life, consider the contributing factors of the spatial triad as a whole. '[T]he act of rhythm analysis integrates these things — this wall, this table, these trees — in a dramatic becoming, in an ensemble full of meaning, transforming them no longer into diverse things, but into presences' (2004, p. 22).

This chapter, then, can be read as an experiment in what happens when the production of space is positioned in opposition to its consumption, and when such intense media scrutiny has shaped the public consciousness to the extent that theatrical and performative theories best explain the spatial dynamics of death and memorial. The infamous anti-memorial is a problematic, performative and deeply contradictory space that represents the theatrical intersections between perceived, conceived and lived space. Infamous places of death often suffer these contradicting performances, and the result is a highly contested lived space. The production of space, in infamous cases such as Cromwell Street, is very much a theatre – either of death or the absence thereof – and in this infamous site of death, it was argued that the *lived* has become a contested, theatrically enacted, space of consumption.

NOTE

1. Refer back to Figure 2.4 in Chapter 2 for a diagram of the arrangement of these aspects of spatial production.

CHAPTER 4

POLITICIZATION (NEUMARKT, DRESDEN)

The previous two chapters employed Lefebvre's conceptual framework on the production of space by exploring its analytical utility in the context of two distinct case studies – the Tyburn site in York and Number 25 Cromwell Street in Gloucester – both of which are easily identified as sites of 'difficult heritage' (Macdonald, 2009) in so far that they represent either a form of State-sponsored violence against its own citizens – in the case of the former – or the notorious activities of two British serial murderers Fred and Rose West – in the case of the latter example. Equally, both sites have been explored through their deviant character, features of which are established in both quality of the acts which make them memorable and in the light of their contested memorialization.

Drawing on the same conceptual framework on the social production of space, this chapter takes a slightly divergent approach in its theoretical analysis, in line with the broader call detailed in earlier chapters for experimentation with regard to the conceptual toolbox we are working towards.

The case study for this chapter considers an event which takes place in Dresden, Germany, namely the annual remembrance of the infamous Bombing of Dresden in World War II: this particular event, observed since 2010, is accompanied by a protest against neo-Nazi marches organised on the same day. In an effort to send a signal to those who would instrumentalise the anniversary of the destruction of the city for far-right propaganda – and to prevent their marches from reaching the historic town centre – thousands of protesters form a human chain around the area. The message is clear, 'let's make Dresden into a peaceful, cosmopolitan stronghold against intolerance and stupidity', as stated by Helma Orosz the major of Dresden when addressing the protestors at the inaugural event in 2010 (Spiegel Online, 2010).

However, rather than focusing on the obvious concerns over far-right marches, in this chapter, I will argue that this memorialization – a human rather than a physical space – should itself be looked at from a more critical perspective. While it would be all too easy to consider it a sign of solidarity and collective political engagement, it is more appropriate to view it in the same light as the so-far fruitless attempts to ban the National Democratic Party of Germany (NPD), a far-right and ultranationalist political party. In other words, in the act of drawing a clear physical border around the historic town centre of Dresden, an ad hoc memorial as much as anything, to prevent far-right marches from entering the area, protestors are doing more than demarcating acceptable and legitimate from illegitimate politics. Rather, they are simultaneously signalling and designating the people involved in such protests as unwanted, redundant and expendable.

To make this point, I will draw on the aspects of Lefebvre's (1991) spatial triad and de Certeau's (1984) concept-city and build on these foundations through more criminological considerations of space and political protest.

The aim here is to highlight the need to think more carefully about the contemporary political landscape, what concerns it deems appropriate and how this dynamic might manifest spatially. In that vein, Lefebvre is deployed not so much to highlight the contested dynamics of socially produced space. In some sense, this would be an obvious point to make given the contradictory nature of Dresden's historical memorialization easily perceived as both perpetrator (i.e. a city in Nazi-Germany) and victim to what has been described as anything from a 'moral crime' (Grayling, 2006) to a 'war crime' (Friedrich, 2002). Instead, I will argue that the spatial triad can also be used to analyse the social production of sanitised, asocial and apolitical space. Simply put, whereas the previous chapters considered scale in relation to physical memorialization and memory, in this chapter, I am seeking to return to Lefebvre's first phase of work (see Chapter 2) on the relationship between the political and the spatial and unpacking some of the ways in which we might understand human agency and action in this context to compliment and contrast the approaches previously developed. This is not meant as an antagonism *per se*, but rather situates Lefebvre's notion of contradictory space from the previous chapter, where we see relationships of 'inclusion and exclusion, conjunction and disjunction' (1991, p. 293), on a human level and augments it with additional supporting evidence and theoretical accounts, thereby broadening the reach of our approach in this book.

4.1. DRESDEN'S NEUMARKT AS CONCEIVED SPACE

Initially, as I have suggested, the political and spatial dynamic described in the previous chapter is not unlike that which I will consider here. We have a publically accessible space which comes with an element of historical baggage and contested heritage, in that it was the sight of death and destruction on that infamous day on 13 February 1945. However, rather than destroying the remnants of suffering, the historic town centre of Dresden was largely reconstructed, with landmark buildings such as the 'Frauenkirche', and the 'Semperoper' (opera house) rebuilt by utilising donations from around the world. In other words, the intention here was to memorialise those who died during the bombing, but given the broader context of this event in World War II, by extension also those who suffered and died as a result of the Nazi regime. Moreover, the reconstruction of Dresden's historic town centre is supposed to add to Germany's broader post- World War II project to reconcile with its past and remind its citizens that such suffering should never be allowed again. The first stage of Lefebvre's (1991) 'spatial triad' is a useful way of understanding this particular city space. The conception of space in the eyes of city planners and social engineers, including those who aspired for Dresden's inner city to be rebuilt in its old design, fits well with Lefebvre's concept of 'conceived space' (or representations of space). Beyond its symbolic purpose to act as a sight of memorialization and reconciliation, an additional benefit of this reconstruction is its role in the local tourism industry. In that sense, Dresden's historic town centre would have been simultaneously conceived as a space of repentance and commercialisation.

For Lefebvre (1991), this is the dominant space conceived by technocratic and administrative processes, in line with the rationalised expectations of spatial dynamics and their role in the mode of production. Lefebvre clearly demarcates this space from the lived experience of usage, but I might also draw on de Certeau (1984) here, who tells us that the actuality of 'walking the city' involves more room for creative freeplay and drift than planners might like or even expect.

Everyday urban life is not sufficiently predictable and uniform in the way that space is used by those walking the city streets. According to the author '[t]heir swarming mass is an innumerable collection of singularities' (p. 97). He explains that the concept of the city is never truly identical to its reality, but rather that the creation of the concept requires the dual ability to think of the real city's plurality and to implement it effectively into the concept-plan. Furthermore, de Certeau (1984, p. 94) is critical of these sorts of administrative processes based on a productive and unitary understanding of the city; this he recognises as the rationalisation of the city which mystifies it in calculations and does so on the basis of the hypothesis of its own destruction. However, one must be careful of this assumed decay of the concept-city as de Certeau makes quite clear in that its failure is not necessarily the failure of the city itself. He proposes that 'the ministers of knowledge' would 'transmute the misfortune of their theories into theories of misfortune' (de Certeau, 1984, p. 96), suggesting that worries of conceptual decay are perhaps being inflated to extend into the condition of the social order as a whole. In other words, screams for increasingly technologically sophisticated strategies of urban control might simply be a desperate attempt to keep going the modernist concept-city.

Building on this, Hayward (2012) suggests that the non-representational theory has the potential to act as a counter-force to these sanitising administrative processes of understanding the city as well as potential violence and destruction in the city in terms of rigid and dehumanising notions of 'hot spots' and 'secure zones'. As discussed in Chapter 2, theories of space can be separated broadly into schools of thought which emphasises on the more or less static geographic account of landscapes, the social construction of space and those which consider space for its relational character. Alternatively, non-representational theory proposes to integrate the material spatial components of studying space, with the more relational aspects of affect, meaning and cultural representation. As such, we might also think through how the dynamics of technocratic rationalisation in the construction Lefebvre's conceived space is itself already the product of social production. In this way, I argue that the human chain set up around the historic town centre of Dresden also operates as a kind of sanitising mechanism to keep out unwanted influences from the far-right and by extension to avoid exposure to the country's historical baggage. We will return to this point at a later stage but for now it suffices to say that the erection of a physical barrier in the form of a human wall of political decency is unlikely to do anything towards the prevention or eradication of far-right extremist movements. Indeed, Hayward (2012) expands on his discussion of non-representational theory, suggesting that it allows us to consider that spaces are more than just geographical locations to be occupied and controlled. He has previously drawn on the experiential and performative dynamic between humans and their relationship with structural and technological artefacts to lead into the notion that space can become parafunctional in the way it is utilised (Hayward, 2004). This is understood as space which seems to have been abandoned by the modernist project and given up on the idea(-l) of determining function through shape. Naturally, local authorities are often wary of such spaces, and are concerned with the relative ambiguity of their meaning and performative practices within it. This intolerance of ambiguity in spatial utility regularly leads to attempts by local authorities to recapture, reshape and reorder such spaces left to choose their own function (ibid.).

The construction of what has been described as 'urban containers' (Jong and Schuilenburg, 2006) is best understood as a contemporary version of medieval-walled towns, which suitably fits the metaphorical message of Dresden's human chain in that it is simultaneously aimed at keeping in as well as out ('inclusive' and 'exclusive' to return to Lefebvre briefly). Contemporary urban life is characterised by a series of encounters with walls, boundaries and perimeters of inclusion and exclusion, which may be entered in a straightforward manner but only in so far as one is not recognised as a threat to the conceived representations of the space itself; I am allowed in because I am the right sort of person in this particular context. In the case of Dresden, it is quite clear that marches by the politically far right are considered tolerable only in so far that they do not occur in the sacred locale of its historic town centre, making this a de facto space of appropriate memorialization.

Of course, the contemporary variant of medieval-walled towns in the form of the 'urban container' no longer demarcates itself from the outside world clearly. Instead, it is scattered across and arguably even between cities. In other words, the inside city no longer protects itself from the outside through perimeter walls, but instead islands of 'urban containers' can be found throughout the city's landscape. To put it in the words of de Jong and Schuilenburg, 'the strict division between the city and the countryside has vanished, dual categories such as "centre" versus "periphery" [...] become obsolete' (2006, p. 45). Here, the 'urban container' exists almost separate from its periphery and even demands a different set of rules from the outside (de Jong and Schuilenburg, 2006, p. 52); such rules would be closely linked to the lifestyle and culture – arguably a manufactured one – of the container. This does not mean, however, that they are devoid of any values. Indeed, de Jong and Schuilenburg argue that this is likely to result in the 'urban containers'' own normative system of behavioural codes which perhaps extend beyond enforcement and conscious obedience. Significantly, unwillingness or inability to obey and accept the protocols will lead to exclusion from the compound itself (de Jong and Schuilenburg, 2006). The authors extend their assessment further in that the 'urban container' no longer concerns itself with concrete threats of crime or violence, but instead concentrates its efforts on excluding risk. At first glance, this might appear to be an effective and worthwhile endeavour, but they also make it quite clear that this is done through increasingly sophisticated surveillance techniques (and technologies) used to identify and remove individuals on the basis of their behaviour alone, at times perhaps relatively mundane and innocent behaviour. This extends the notion of Lefebvre's conceived space in potentially disturbing ways, blocking out dissent through the remit of planning-in some groups and excluding others based on particular preferences.

When applying this to Dresden's annual protest against far-right marches entering the historic town centre, we might say that the risk of symbolic invasion of the space's remit as a place of remorse and reconciliation constitutes the real focus of the human chain. Fundamentally, the normative conception of this place of 'difficult heritage' is defined very narrowly without facilitating the political voices of those who would conceive of it otherwise. While it would clearly be inappropriate to claim a moral equivalence between Nazi-Germany's atrocities and the excessive Bombing of Dresden as highlighted earlier, it is not uncommon for the latter to be described as anything from a 'moral crime' to a 'war crime'. Thus, the memorialization of Dresden's historic town centre as the historical victim of excessive violence in war should be included in the broader political narrative, especially given that it is all too easy for far-right movements to instrumentalised. As such, drawing on the non-representational theory's integrated approach, it is possible to conceive of the human chain as more than simply a material barrier between the centre and periphery, but as a socially produced material, spatial, as well as normative system which is relational in its engagement with physical space and other humans, as much as it is affective and fuelled by the emotive sensations of the event.

4.2. DRESDEN'S NEUMARKT AS PERCEIVED SPACE

Moving on from Lefebvre's 'conceived space' to the 'perceived space' described by de Certeau (1984) as the actuality of 'walking the city', it might be said that the human chain is a symbolic as well as physical mechanism for keeping political life out of the historically significant town centre of Dresden. Considering the sensitive nature of this space, both in terms of history and politics, it is unsurprising that far-right protesters would aspire to enter into that same space for their political voices to be heard. Albeit at times in a disruptive manner, before 2010, when Dresden's mayor Helma Orosz called for the first human chain protest, far-right nationalists frequently engaged in their own practices of commemoration each year (von Borries, 2015). However, even debates over whether this would inappropriately legitimate extreme and hyper-nationalist views are largely muted in the celebration of those who come together to perform their own individual acts of mourning and repentance while standing hand-in-hand.

That said, the issue to address here is not the act of protesting against far-right marches or commemorating those who died as a result of Nazi-Germany's atrocities. Instead, we might consider the symbolic purpose and effect of the human chain in respect of sociological explanations for the rise of the right across Europe and the Western world. For example, I can see from a publication on English nationalism and the transformation of working class politics which came out only last year, that the flattened-out nature of our political landscape and its longstanding shift away from class politics to identity politics, has resulted in antagonistic attitudes towards the political 'centre' stemming from a sense of being totally ignored by mass-mediated culture (Winlow et al., 2017). The authors of that piece make a strong case for a renewed leftist discourse concentrated on advocating for economic security, collectivism, equality and community protection, and the need to announce those principles across the social landscape, including the education system and mass media. In this context, the symbolic purpose of the human chain shows both the inclusivity of collective action and colectivised closing-out of an alternative debate, regardless of how unpalatable that debate might be.

But how can the dynamics that inform the protest against far-right marches by the political 'centre' in Germany relate with the spatial triad here? Lefebvre describes representational space 'as directly *lived* through its associated images and symbols, and hence the space of "inhabitants" and "users"' (1991, p. 39, original emphasis). Watkins (2005) elaborates on this in highlighting that it is the space which overlays onto the physical space as it is lived in everyday life. As such, it is in the realm of representational lived space that diversity, deviation and individuality are constructed and cultivated. Moreover, it is precisely this aspect of unpredictable infiltration which is essential in the possibility for social encounters. In that sense, successful social interactions are achieved in conjunction with, although not fully repressed by, the constraining features of representations of space (Watkins, 2005). Of course, in the case of Dresden, I am speaking here not of architectural or topographical arrangements alone, which partially inhibit and interact with the lived imposition of representational space, but am suggesting also that conceived space itself is already (and perhaps, arguably, primarily) symbolic in light of the fact that much of the space's significance – while deriving from the post-World War II restoration – is culturally construed. However, the key point to make here concerns the dual proposition that 'inhabitants' and 'users' are essential in the generation of lived space, and that their infiltration into the predictable nature of the conceived representations of space works as prerequisites for social encounters and the production of social space as such: interaction is prefigured environmentally, which in turn, loops around to restrict the design of future conceived spaces.

Looking at it this way, the human chain that is formed around Dresden's historic town centre as part of a protest against far-right marches entering into that space, can be considered a reaction to the risk of physical as well as symbolic infiltration, but in the act of creating a physical barrier between desirable and undesirable 'inhabitants' and 'users', this simultaneously removes the possibility for social encounters to occur. As such, it may be necessary to consider whether the analytical potential of Lefebvre's spatial triad should be reduced to considerations of the production of 'social' space. Alternatively, I suggest that, for spatial theory to remain fruitful, it needs to allow for the possibility of 'the production of social space', which may be described as *asocial*.

Considering Massey's (1993) discussion of the increasing interconnectedness between people and places (see Chapter 2), it is necessary to consider that the way space is governed depends largely on the relations of power and control which permeate through spatial arrangements, the symbolic conception of space and the lived representation of space. Who is allowed to enter Dresden's historic town centre and participate in the production of social space is equally restrictive and as such the notion that it is in fact fully 'social' space is problematic. If space does indeed frame social action, then the expulsion of far-right political activity constitutes a manner of asocial and apolitical disengagement, which has been described by some as the cynical wisdom of 'capitalist realism' (Fisher, 2009).

In *Capitalist Realism*, Fisher describes an ideological dynamic whereby 'beliefs have collapsed at the level of ritual or symbolic elaboration, and all that is left is the consumer-spectator, trudging through the ruins and the relics' (ibid., p. 4). This means that the cultural and political landscape has moved from belief to aesthetics and from engagement to spectatorship, bringing with it attitudes of ironic distance immune to the seductions of fanaticism remembered from past eras of terror and totalitarianism. This fear, of what Oakeshott (1996) came to describe as 'barbarism of order', seems to inform much of the spatial-political dynamics which occur in Dresden annually on 13 February. Building on this idea, Hall argues that 'post-war liberal thought has generated a fear of "barbarism of order" that is so strong and pervasive that the "barbarism of disorder" is offered up as that which is to be tolerated as the least worst option' (2012, p. 250). Moreover, the cynical acceptance regarding politics and belief described by both Fisher and Hall is not a call in committed support for the status quo, nor is it a clear articulation of consensus. Instead, as Hall (2012) explains, it is driven by the fear that the eruption of fear of the barbarism of disorder (e.g. among far-right groups and movements) will lead to a new age of State terror and totalitarian regimes resembling those of the twentieth century. In that sense, the human chain should be seen as an attempt to keep the 'barbarians at the gate' (Hall and Winlow, 2004).

The political and cultural dynamic described above, characterised by ironic distance from beliefs – political or otherwise – can be observed in a similar manner in the light of the socio-spatial logic of the human chain. Just as medieval towns would have been surrounded by walls for protection against physical threats from the outside, contemporary life is often organised by 'container spaces' scattered across the urban landscape. Following on from my earlier discussion on this scattered phenomenon, the human chain might be described as a temporary node in an array of 'shielded mobilities' (Atkinson, 2008). Atkinson uses this idea to explain the lives of the super-rich in a 'plutocratic cloud' with fortified or gated homes and places of work, but it can also apply here in the social production of a human shield against the physical and symbolic invasion of 'unsanitary' political beliefs. This idea can be augmented with Sibley's (1995) argument that feelings about what kinds of people belong in a space can have a profound effect on the way social space is shaped (potentially echoed in Fuller's account of housing design from Chapter 2). In this sense, the human chain can be described as a socially produced phenomenon of 'spatial purification' (Sibley, 1995).

What is presented as protest against the risk of far-right marches entering Dresden's historic town centre appears more accurately as a socio-spatial manifestation of political purification. As much as it may also be laudable that thousands of people would come together to protest, it is telling that it is not organised in support of any particular political system of belief or set of realisable principles for political and economic restructuring. Instead, the event is understood as a counterforce to the rising tide of far-right marches threatening to appear on the doorsteps of Dresden's Neumarkt. Of course, such programmes of public closure cannot be realised quite so concretely but must be disguised as something else. It is here, where the concept of 'quality of life' crimes aids as the main thrust in justifying exclusivity to restore and revitalised the so-called public good (Ferrell, 2001). If Lefebvre

(1991) is correct in suggesting that social space is produced, then the lived conception of Dresden's historic town centre with the organisation of a human chain as a blockading protest against far-right marches is producing a more exclusive, uniform and unifunctional space where other aspects of the spatial triad are significantly diminished.

This leads me back to the conceptual utility of the 'urban container'. While town centres are rarely if ever enclosed they certainly do have their own normative systems of behaviour (de Jong and Schuilenburg, 2006). Building on this, George Ritzer's *McDonaldization* thesis, or more specifically his socio-geographic image of the islands of the living dead, can be used to add to Lefebvre's broader spatial corpus. Ritzer has written extensively on his updated version of Weberian rationalisation, where contemporary society is understood to increasingly put into place processes to ensure maximum efficiency, calculability, predictability and control (2011). With this concept in mind, Ritzer (2003) sets himself the task of formulating an image of social geography which could describe the McDonaldization phenomenon in a realistic fashion. Due to McDonaldization's origin in Weber's rationalisation paradigm, it is no surprise that Ritzer (ibid.) would have started by considering the image of the 'iron cage'. However, he soon realised that such an understanding of rationalisation is far too all encompassing to be a realistic representation. He further notes that this is hardly surprising due to Weber's preference for concentrating on specific institutions; this suggests that Weber was in actuality picturing a series of iron cages rather than one that is omnipresent. While Ritzer (2003) believes that an iron cage of rationalisation is certainly a possibility in the future, for the time being he considers that it would be far more effective to think in terms of islands of rationalisation, to add to our spatial corpus. Perhaps naturally, this leads him to consider Foucault's 'carceral archipelago', but he ultimately concludes that these present a much too restricted sense of being enclosed and inescapability.

Following these theoretical avenues, Ritzer (ibid.) proposes the phantasmagorical social geographic image of 'islands of the living dead' and explains that such islands of rationalised death are still relatively far apart while life and death co-exist in a paradoxical relationship within these islands. In other words, while islands of rationalisation are 'settings in which large portions of life have come to be confined' (ibid., p. 127), it cannot be ignored that much living still goes on within them. Similar to container spaces, living on these islands is clearly separated from living on the outside, a type of ghettoisation of life, and in the case considered here, politics. In Dresden, this homogenisation of social and political life is established in the practised spatial manifestation of the human chain. Ritzer (ibid.) acknowledges a conflict between the human actor's tendency to create life and with it unpredictability and uncontrollability and those in charge of minimising it, although what he might not have considered fully is the degree to which public subjectivities are also shaped by the implementation of sanitising and fortifying practices in what might otherwise constitute a fully social space. Drawing on the criminological theory for a moment, Raymen (2016) points to the formation of asocial subjectivities in the light of situational crime prevention strategies intended and designed initially to 'design out crime' from urban environments. However, not only do these often fail to achieve their chosen objective of preventing crime (Hayward, 2012), they can actively contribute to the perpetuation and exacerbation of those very subjectivities which fuel motivations for crime and selfish destructiveness. The human chain around the historic town centre of Dresden can be understood in a similar manner in so far that together with the symbolic understanding of the space (the perceived), it constitutes a series of spatial practices which reflect subjectivities in line with a politics framed by the fear of a 'barbarism of order'.

4.3. SPATIAL PRACTICE AND POLITICAL SUBJECTIVITIES

We can speak here of Lefebvre's spatial practice in the same way that Jodi Dean discusses 'communicative capitalism' as 'the materialisation of ideals of inclusion and participation in information, entertainment, and communication technologies in ways that capture resistance and intensify global capitalism' (2009, p. 2). While Lefebvre describes spatial practice as emerging from the dynamic interplay of spatial configurations, the lived but increasingly codified conception of Dresden's historic town centre — through the implementation of the human chain — indicates something more in line with a loss of the 'right to the city' (Lefebvre, 1967). As Harvey (2012) explains Lefebvre's concept of the 'right to the city' stands for more than the ability of individuals to access its resources and services. Instead, it is a broader, more collective right to change ourselves and our society by changing the city and its processes of urbanisation. However, Dresden's human chain does not enact this right nor is it a cause to speak of attempts to reclaim public space. Instead, its spatial practice perpetuates a kind of retreat into individualistic self-interests and captured resistance under 'communicative capitalism'.

A plethora of literature already exists which deals with withdrawal from public life driven by a fear of the Other and a sense that the stranger represents an external threat rather than standing for the potential source of social engagement (Simmel, 1908, for a classic example of this). This is more recently researched with reference to the wealthy who have been identified as shielding themselves from public life and dangerous encounters with the Other (Atkinson et al., 2016; Webber and Burrows, 2016). The rich are said to organise their lives within a network of 'shielded mobilities', which works to constitute a wider 'plutocratic cloud' (Atkinson, 2008). However, similar dynamics can be observed more broadly in the general retreat from public life in our cities. While rarely empty, the contemporary urban landscape is arguably deprived of social interaction and social space (Sennett, 1977). This is most clearly observed in the manner in which people generally rush through city centres, constantly mobile and only stopping to enter retail stores or to engage in any number of consumer activities – according to Ritzer '[t]he ideal would be consumers [are those] who move through the system quickly and efficiently' (2003, p. 134) – but moving away from the obvious focus on consumer culture and its spatial manifestation in the urban landscape, it is more important to point out here that a similar dynamic can be seen in regards to political activism and political engagement as well as how this manifests spatially.

To augment Lefebvre's spatial approach in the light of the episodic character of Dresden's annual anti-far-right protest, I am reminded of Murray Bookchin's (1995) damning diagnosis of trends in political activism since the 1970s, which he came to describe as 'lifestyle anarchism'. In his analysis, he identified a number of trends some of which can be directly related to Dresden's annual human chain. To begin with, he noticed a move towards protests which more closely resembled episodic events lacking a clear political programme and plan for action. The second trend is perhaps best described as a move towards protests motivated by 'instrumental reason' (Horkheimer, 1974), whereby the protest itself becomes the goal rather than a means to achieving a more or less well-defined political vision. Hence, the lack of a meaningful agenda for political change ensures that the movement itself is all that remains. Third, Bookchin identified the absence of a universalist political vision under which people with diverse backgrounds may organise to push for wide-ranging changes. While there are more trends that I could focus on here, for the purposes of this chapter, these three will suffice to make a number of critical points about the nature of Dresden's annual protest and its spatially practised manifestation.

The fact that the human chain has now become an annual occurrence rather than a coherent programme, which may work to prevent the rise of far-right movements on the level of political engagement is telling in so far that it seems, for the most part, to work as an opportunity for participants to choose their own cause and do so in socially producing an enclosed space. As such, media representations of the protests make frequent reference to the diversity of motivations for people to join in the protest, echoing the sort of symbolic order discussed in the previous chapter. This is an interesting observation, given that Bookchin (1995) identified a trend in social movements characterised by a move away from reason and towards relativist, subjective and, by extension, emotive motivations for political activism. In the same sense, Dresden's protest is not seen as an instrument *for* change but as the instrument *of* change. Of course, the protest does not produce any change in the attitudes of far-right and neo-Nazi groups nor can the event be considered change in and of itself. Instead, in the contemporary political landscape, it is simply seen as enough that protestors are able to express their own individual(ist) feelings of remorse, repentance and any number of political sentiments including those against the far-right through the frame of Dresden's historic town centre and what it represents as a conflicting site of memorialization: what we have here is a spatially configured manifestation of a loss to the 'right to the city', as conceptualised earlier.

Finally, this leads me to Bookchin's third diagnosis that social movements since the 1970s have increasingly drifted away from engaging with universalist political ideals. Indeed it seems that much of what is on offer in terms of participation in the political landscape presents itself as the politics of identity, diversity and individual difference. As such, politics itself becomes a lifestyle choice. This is where Dresden's annual human chain protest against far-right marches comes to its full (negative) potential in that the nature of this event stands entirely for the consensus politics of cosmopolitan multiculturalism with little regard for class political considerations. The protest does not present an alternative political programme with universal principles of collectivism, economic security and equality, but rather more accurately constitutes a continuation of the 'denazification' programmes instituted in both East and West Germany after World War II, and subsequently memorializes and legitimises this practice in the process.

Importantly, even in their immediate implementation during the post-war era, these programmes were met with the reality that those who did not obviously benefit from the Nazi regime and had no direct involvement in the killing of minorities more often than not saw themselves as victims instead of perpetrators (Winlow et al., 2015). Moving forward to the twenty-first century, it is not surprising that many in Germany, including some who have joined in on far-right activism in Dresden, would see themselves as victims, both of the political status quo of cosmopolitan consensus politics and, by means of historical symbolism and alternative memorialization, of the city's bombing on 13 February 1945. This means that the human chain takes up a particular role in the spatial configuration of subjectivities which represents the state of the current political landscape and its anti-utopian preference for piecemeal reform.

Ultimately, the annual human chain protest in Dresden against neo-Nazi marches is similar to the rise of far-right movements across Europe and the Western world, in that they should be considered as two sides of the same coin, lacking the courage to organise for systemic political change. Moreover, their engagement as either regressive nationalists or lifestyle activists (Sotirakopoulos, 2016) means that their theatrical expressions (see Chapter 3) offer little more than a kind of pantomime. While the far-right organizes marches, the infantilized political 'centre' engages in similar episodic protests ultimately failing at the point of offering a meaningful counter-movement and taking on its own regressive role as the infantilized audience which shouts back (Hayward, 2012) from the spatially practised enclosure of Dresden's historic town centre.

4.4. CONCLUSION

What is being proposed in this chapter is threefold. Firstly, Lefebvre's spatial triad as a framework for the analysis of spatial production can be moved and shifted to fit an analysis which recognizes social production already at the stage of conceived space. While Dresden's historic town centre represents a symbolic conception of memorialization, mourning and cultural and historical significance, given the episodic nature of the human chain protest, it is necessary to conceive of this stage of representations of space as already lived. The historic town centre is not simply conceived – followed by the infiltration of life – but space itself can take on a situational character whereby it is not independent of its original symbolism, but becomes transmuted as an event-based conceived space: our understanding of this space of memorialization is framed by these competing political narratives. Indeed, drawing on the influence of non-representational theory, such an integrated approach is beneficial in considering both relational and representational aspects of space, but also its situational dynamic and ensuing event sensations so as to make sense of how this space is configured and reconfigured each year.

Secondly, representational space as the encounter between conceived space and life is not so easily separated from symbolic or administrative conceptions. Much has been written about the erection of walls and the demarcation of securitised perimeters in the contemporary urban landscape, but little consideration is given to this dynamic occurring on the level of social interaction or in the context of situational barriers. In this analysis, the annual human chain protest around the historic town centre of Dresden works as an agent of conceived space that is both temporally concentrated and socially constituted. Moreover, there is a distinct political character to this particular dynamic of a socially produced space, akin to Lefebvre's early focus more than his later work; the human chain prevents both physically and metaphorically any real potential at political engagement with the underlying sociopolitical causes for the surge of far-right movements. I argue here that this is symptomatic of a fear since the end of World War II that a new 'barbarism of order' will emerge out of the increasing disorder in our contemporary social and political landscape. Unfortunately, the erection of this particular barrier constitutes little more than an attempt to keep the 'barbarians at the gate', denying in one sense their right to the city (Lefebvre, 1967).

The nature of political activism and subjectivities which are presented here is one of fear and cynicism. My reading of the human chain protest in Dresden fits with a broader critique of social movements since the 1970s. Its lack of a coherent political programme means that the event itself is more episodic than transformative. Given this obvious limitation at what is supposedly a political event, it is perhaps unsurprising that reports on the protest are dominated by references to protestors' diverse and personal motivations for participating; this goes a long way to show the relativist, subjective and emotive dimension of this event, as these fill the void of a space that might otherwise be occupied by concrete socio-political and structural contestation. This reading also chimes with the sorts of issues identified in Chapter 3 around the role of the media in developing and maintaining particular forms of symbolic order, which in turn frames the event and reinforces the perceived significance of it in the eyes of others.

Thirdly, with this emphasis on subjective experience and motivation, the protest is characterised by the cynical logic of instrumental reason. Put simply, the human chain is not used as an instrument for, but considered to be the instrument *of* change itself. The abandonment of universalist political ideals has created a situation where protests such as the one in Dresden are characterised by the consensus politics of cosmopolitan multiculturalism with little regard for other class political considerations: this, I have argued, is effectively a new way of understanding the relationship between conceived and perceived space, with town planners replaced by a policing of symbolic political arrangements within a specific locale. Rather than engage the far-right and those who participate in their marches in an open debate over policy and principles, protest takes on a seemingly theatrical character, with the human chain representing the sort of 'dramatic action' discussed in Chapter 3. While economic and political realities are increasingly defined by new conditions of disorder, the only available response to the regressive surge of far-right movements seems to be one of an infantilised political 'centre' engaging in episodes of protest and 'shouting back', but ultimately failing to produce an alternative political programme based on universal principles and ideals. In doing so, the interrelated nature of the spatial triad is stymied by one dominant approach, and our engagement with the dynamism and potentiality for agentic action becomes severely curtailed or, worse still, entirely prescribed by forces beyond our control.

CONCLUSIONS

We started this book by contextualising some of the rhetoric surrounding what can be done with 'deviant spaces', particularly those where we find the conflicting demands of community, consumption and politics – 'do we just toss them into the ash bin of history, purging them as if they never existed?' (Glaser, 2017, p. 1). It is a question that we did not seek to answer directly, but instead we sought to explore how the multifarious agendas of different agents could be understood through spatial theory, particularly Lefebvre's spatial triad, as outlined in Chapter 3. From there, we used three escalating case studies of Tyburn in York, Number 25 Cromwell Street in Gloucester and the historic town centre of Dresden to explore how memorialization (formal and informal, as well as the lack thereof) 'works' in terms of how the spaces are physically and socially constructed and articulated. In each chapter, we have applied aspects of Lefebvre's spatial triad to the sites of death, and expanded that framework to draw upon complimentary and contrasting elements of Lefebvre's broader corpus of work, including under-utilised conceptual approaches in *The Production of Space* (1991), as well as *Writings on Cities* (1996) and *Rhythmanalysis* (2004); in doing so, we have aimed to demonstrate the continuing vibrancy and versatility of Lefebvre's work as applied to a series of scalar cases, responding to Harvey's (2015) call for creative scale-based readings of alternative heritage spaces.

In the introduction, we outlined three questions for this book to grapple with – so it makes sense to address them sequentially. Initially, we wanted to build some conceptual tools that could help us to understand the relationship between spatial interests, local (community) consequences and the memorialization of infamous death. In our discussion of theoretical discussions of space, we initially justified our hodgepodge approach to Lefebvre through Deleuze (2007) and Strathern (2005): this book is an assemblage of potential applications, partial connections and subjective knowledge. In part, this meant we could respond to the concerns of Jessop et al. (2008, p. 391) that, historically speaking, place-based approaches have tended to treat spaces as 'discrete, more or less self-contained, more or less self-identical ensembles'. We treated this as a springboard to suggest that any usable spatial theory would have to take account of both the scale and (ir)regular, interconnected tempo of urban life that Lefebvre terms 'rhythms'. Following on from previous research concerning dark tourism and difficult heritage, the approach would also have to go beyond the usual method of categorising how space is conceived and extend to how it is actually used to properly unpack the conflicting demands of consumption, community and politics.

To this end and as a way of moving closer to Waterton and Watson's (2013) call for a 'critical imagination' in the study of heritage, we found Lefebvre's spatial triad – and his connected concepts of theatrics and contradiction – to be especially useful. Through Lefebvre, it was possible to piece together the conflicting aspects of all three sites as they are produced socially.

At the first site, Tyburn (York), we found a conceived space that is understated to the extent that the presence of a memorial is often unclear — save for an information plaque, a concrete plinth and a bench. The lived space of Tyburn, on the other hand, was just as much a part of the flows of contemporary urban life today as it was a space for spectacle in its former life as gallows; only now, the context is clearly wildly different. We used its interstitial position — between a racecourse and a main road, nestled in a wooded area crisscrossed by a winding network of pathways — to advocate for Lefebvre's lesser-used concept of 'theatrical space' as part of our conceptual framework for understanding deviant memorials. Here, we started with Lefebvre's (1991, p. 188) definition of the theatre, where we see the 'interplay between fictitious and real counterparts and its interaction between gazes and mirages in which actor, audience, "characters", text, all come together but never become one'. We interpreted these intersections of 'fictitious and real' through the context of the space, the presence of various sites of information and symbolism, alongside the formal memorials dramatising particular members of 'celebrity dead' such as Richard 'Dick' Turpin, and the informal memorials to those members of the public who have enjoyed the space more recently (not to forget the literal, historical performance of execution also embodied within the concrete platform of the memorial space itself).

At the second site, Number 25 Cromwell Street (Gloucester), we reinterpreted theatrics to account for a space that has endured sustained and unsavoury media attention. Theatrics, at the Cromwell Street walkway, can be understood through countless hours of media attention — in the form of news and popular culture — and the impact this has had in framing this space as a site of death and deviance rather than a community space, a place of residence and definitely not as a memorial. In this chapter, we used the Cromwell Street case study as an example of what we termed 'anti-memorial' — where the conceived space is framed deliberately in opposition to any sort of remembrance and in hostility towards the aforementioned media coverage. We argued that this is reflective of Lefebvre's comments on the contradiction and contestation of the spaces of production and spaces of consumption. Despite a conceived antagonism towards dark tourism and a conceived space that is oppositional to consumption – the walkway is very much a consumed space – from the consumption of tourist experiences to the consumption of criminal celebrities, and the voyeuristic gaze of the news media that have facilitated both.

The third site, Dresden (Germany), allowed us to explore how the politicisation of a particular space – in this case, the historic town centre that was rebuilt following the end of World War II – can be framed as a quasi- or anti-memorial in an entirely embodied sense through the human chain. This space was also contested and could be read as an anti-memorial in one sense through the protest against the far-right, but also as a problematised space for memorialization for the far right. The particular political positioning of anti-fascist protest in this case study favours, as we have suggested, an approach that seeks to diminish particular narratives in favour of others, so the deeply held beliefs of some groups – including neo-Nazis – who advocate for this space as representative of a war crime rather than the rebuilding of Germany on a symbolic level, show an ongoing contestation enacted through the conceived (the planned-out reconstruction of the space and what it should be used for) and the perceived (the symbolic resonance of the space). Moving forward, further exploring the lived dimensions of this space outside the theatricality of the human chain would allow us to test the usability of our framework on a larger scale.

Now to answer our second question: how do local communities negotiate 'difficult heritage' under these circumstances? We conclude that a framework for understanding this has to be necessarily open and flexible to account for the interplay of different social forces on and in the space. Difficult heritage, when allowing for scale, and particularly when scaled down, is manifold: as it is lived, difficult heritage can manifest itself in the tawdry world of souvenir hunting 'dark tourists', or through the actions of local residents simply worried about the depreciation of their property assets (and anything and everything in between); the challenge then is to offer ways of thinking through these spaces that avoid reductivism, while also remaining coherent enough to be useful.

In Tyburn, the York City Council has chosen an understated memorial to those executed by the State, but this is arguably permissible owing to the passage of time. As we noted, very few people who use the site on a daily basis engage with the less palatable aspects of the history of the gallows, showing the crucial role that 'lived' space plays in the co-production of the social world. On the other hand, with the more recent and gruesome nature of what went on at Number 25 Cromwell Street, Gloucester Council is not afforded the same ease of preservation; difficult heritage in the consumed space, saturated with media attention, was counteracted with the absence of any memorial at all. Thirdly, in Dresden, we thought about a more traditional type of difficult heritage but with a very different type of memorial — the non-fixed 'human chain' around the town centre, which has seen thousands of people congregate in both an act of remembrance and political defiance (or capitulation depending on your perspective), rather than consumption. In this instance, memorial is met with a divergent anti-memorial to that seen in Cromwell Street: far-right and neo-Nazi marches that contest one conception of Dresden as somewhere rebuilt for remembrance in favour of the site of a perceived war crime in the Allied bombing of the city in the closing stages of World War II.

By contrast, anti-memorial in Gloucester could be interpreted as Lefebvre's 'conceived' space, in Dresden it is the 'perceived' space of symbolic meaning that has worked together in anti-memorialization against the beliefs of far-right and neo-Nazi groups in the community. We argued that local communities primarily negotiate difficult heritage through the interlinking of the conceived, perceived and lived aspects which produce social space.

Third, and finally, we asked: what is the context for the interplay and conflicting demands of 'difficult heritage', 'dark tourism' and 'memorialization' through space? Although our case studies have been disparate and different when it comes to size, geography and type, the most appropriate way to understand the context of these contestations through Lefebvre is his concept of 'contradictory space'. Or rather, the theoretical openness that is afforded to us when we see memorials as formed by a myriad of physical, social and governmental forces — some of which exist in perpetual states of contradiction. In this way, it is possible for us to respond to the concerns of Jessop et al. (2008) about reducing space to particular typologies: instead of looking at memorials to the difficult dead as discrete, physical entities we have argued that they instead constituted at the intersection of conceived, perceived and lived space. They are socially produced.

C.1. WHERE NEXT?

We hope that researchers and students in dark tourism and difficult heritage, or death studies more generally, will read this book as an experimental foray into testing and applying a spatial theoretical framework to infamous memorial. We have done so in a way that incorporates memorials of different types, scales and times — and encourage you to do the

Conclusions

same. Those who apply frameworks to things are often doing so in a way that allows very little room for interpretation. Philip Stone's 'dark tourism spectrum' (2006) comes to mind when looking for a skeleton that is very useful for highlighting the breadth and scale of a discipline area, but is near impossible to *use* when no site seems to fit into one discrete category. This, on the other hand, is a scaffold about how spaces are used, that was built to be used. It accounts for the multifarious, conflicting and overlapping forces at play in the social construction of memorial while allowing interpretation and not shying away from contradiction.

We have treated our cases as three parts of a deliberately disparate whole, but each one has its own narrative that can only be complimented by further field work that tests our initial scalar premise. Tyburn alludes to the importance of theatrics, and particularly, how theatrics are made more complicated by the passage of time and the changing practical use(s) of space. It would be interesting to see how ideas developed in this chapter could apply to other examples where, for instance, the growing city has come to reshape the use of space and the subsequent memorialization of formerly acceptable practices such as routine execution; similarly, the juxtaposition of formal and informal memorialization problematises the conceived understanding of what a memorial should be. Comparing and contrasting the experience at Tyburn with other sites would strengthen the value of theatrical space as a way of thinking through intersectional uses of this type of memorials.

Building on this, Number 25 Cromwell Street speaks to the spaces of contested consumption and considers how a contradictory memorial space can sit between that of production and consumption. It would be interesting to see how this Lefebvrian critique could be applied to, for example, the highly contested 'dark tourist' space that is London's *Jack the*

Ripper Museum on Cable Street: this space was billed — according to its planning application — as a museum for the historical plight of women in London's East End, only for it to become apparent-upon-reveal that the lens through which the curators had chosen to do this was the 'celebrified', an almost mythical character of the infamous Whitechapel serial killer. The use of this space to glorify crime as well as the disingenuous way in which it came into being and the resultant community outrage could perhaps be investigated as a further example of a contradictory, theatrical site of consumption that overlaps with memorial. Additionally, there are potential overlaps with the work of Ruth Penfold-Mounce in terms of the normalisation of sites of death and consumption that could be further explored (2016, 2018).

Dresden comes closest to directly engaging with the quote that acts to bookend our work here, namely how America is presently grappling with the contested symbolic nature of Civil War statues, their historical value and their ongoing association with deeply troubling undertones of racism and segregation in the USA. Perhaps the themes explored in this chapter about the conceived and perceived voices of anti-memorial could be extended to think through protests across the Atlantic that have seen some of the last remaining confederate flags removed from State buildings and memorials to once lauded generals pulled down and destroyed. Regardless of our personal politics towards the misguided actions of far-right apologists, there is a broader issue at stake here in terms of who is permitted to speak and who is not, and this echoes wider issues of power and control that we initially introduced through the work of Massey (1993, 1994, 2013) in Chapter 2. One of the key debates in heritage remains who speaks for whom, and perhaps in unpacking and applying Lefebvre's notions of space, we have moved closer to understanding the complexity of this.

Conclusions

We started this book by situating what we wanted to do as perched somewhere between social and relation readings of space. The book has been written in response to Harvey's concerns about scale in heritage (2015), and throughout the book we have used an intentionally adaptable conceptual framework to address not only this issue but also as a way of avoiding the pitfalls of conforming too close to predominant schools of thought, either in dark tourism studies or in spatial theory itself. The result – which we hope has been of interest if nothing else – is a theoretical hodgepodge (Deleuze, 2007), a laying-out of conceptual tools for further work. However, it is also an intervention, one that shows the true value of creative approaches to Lefebvrian theories of space and towards our understanding of the complexity of relations between memorialization, deviant spaces and the 'difficult dead'.

BIBLIOGRAPHY

Anon. 2007. *Cranntara*. [Online] Available at: https://cranntara.scot/york.htm [Accessed 12 04 2018].

Anon. 2010. *Dresden Stemmt Sich Gegen die Geschichtsklitterer*. [Online] Available at: http://www.spiegel.de/politik/deutschland/zehntausend-bei-anti-neonazi-kette-dresden-stemmt-sich-gegen-die-geschichtsklitterer-a-677692.html [Accessed 12 02 2018].

Anon. n.d. *West Murders*. [Online] Available at: http://gloucestershirepolicearchives.org.uk/content/moving-with-the-times/crime-and-criminals/west-murders [Accessed 12 04 2018].

Antze, P. and Lambek, M. 1996. *Tense Past*. New York, NY: Routledge.

Appropriate Adult. 2011. [Film] Directed by Julian Jarrold. s.l.: s.n.

Atkinson, R. 2008. Commentary: Gentrification, Segregation and the Vocabulary of Affluent Residential choice, *Urban Studies*, 45(12), 2626–2636.

Atkinson, R., Burrows, R. and Rhodes, D. 2016. Capital City? London's Housing Markets and the 'Super-Rich'. In *Handbook on Wealth and the Super-Rich*, Eds. I. Hay and J. Beaverstock, Cheltenham, Edward Elgar Publishing.

Barton, A. and Brown, A. 2015. Show Me the Prison: The Development of Prison Tourism in the UK, *Crime, Media, Culture*, 11(3), 237–258.

Bookchin, M. 1995. *Social Anarchism or Lifestyle Anarchism: An Unbridgeable Chasm*, Edinburgh, AK Press.

Bottomley, C. 2010. *The Tyburn on Knavesmire Set for a Makeover*. [Online] Available at: http://www.yorkpress.co.uk/news/8370035.York_gallows_set_for_a_makeover/ [Accessed 12 12 2017].

Bourdieu, P. 1984. *Distinction*, Cambridge, MA, Harvard University Press.

Braithwaite, D. and Lee, Y.L. 2006. Dark Tourism, Hate and Reconciliation: The Sandakan Experience, *International Institute for Peace Through Tourism*, 8.

Brenner, N. and Elden, S. 2009. Henri Lefebvre on State, Space, Territory, *International Political Sociology*, 3(4), 353–377.

Broughton, S. 1900. *The True and Illustrated Chronicles of the Last Man Gibbetted in Yorkshire*. s.l.: Imprint Unknown.

Castells, M. and Sheridan, A. 1977. The Urban Question: A Marxist Approach. *Social Structure and Social Change*, 1.

Clark, G. and Clark, A. 2001. Common Rights to Land in England, *The Journal of Economic History*, 61(4), 1009–1036.

Cote, J. 2009. Postcolonial Shame: Heritage and the Forgotten Pain of Civilian Women Internees in Java. In *Places of Pain and Shame: Dealing with 'Difficult Heritage'*, Abingdon, Routledge.

Dann, G. 1994. Tourism: The Nostalgia Industry of the Future, In *Global Tourism: the Next Decade*, Oxford, Butterworth.

de Certeau, M. 1984. *The Practice of Everyday Life*, Berkeley, CA, University of California Press.

de Jong, A. and Schuilenburg, M. 2006. *Mediapolis: Popular Culture and the City*, Rotterdam, nai010 publishers.

Dean, J. 2009. *Democracy and Other Neoliberal Fantasies: Communicative Capitalism and Left Politics*, Durham, NC, Duke University Press.

Deleuze, G. 2007. *Two Regimes of Madness: Texts and Interviews 1975–1995 MIT*, Cambridge, CA, The MIT Press.

Denham, J. 2016. The Commodification of the Criminal Corpse: 'Selective Memory' in Posthumous Representations of Criminal, *Mortality*, 21(3), 229–245.

Douglas, M. 1982. *Cultural Bias. In the Active Voice*, London, Routledge.

Dourish, P. 2006. *Re-space-ing Place: Place and Space Ten Years On, ACM*, pp. 299–308.

Duclos, D. and Pingree, A. 1998. *The Werewolf Complex: America's Fascination with Violence*, Oxford, Berg.

Durkheim. 1915. *The Elementary Forms of Religious Life: A Study in Religious Sociology*, London, George Allen.

Elias, N. 1978. *What is Sociology?* New York, NY, Columbia University Press.

Emirbayer, M. 1997. Manifesto for a Relational Sociology, *American Journal of Sociology*, 103(2), 281–317.

Esposito, E. 2008. Social Forgetting: A Systems-Theory Approach. In *Cultural Memory Studies: An International and Interdisciplinary Handbook*, Eds A. Erll and A. Nünning, Berlin, Walter de Gruyter.

Ferguson, E. 2004. *There's Nobody Home*. [Online] Available at: https://www.theguardian.com/uk/2004/feb/15/ukcrime.prisonsandprobation [Accessed 12 8 2017].

Ferrell, J. 2001. *Tearing Down The Streets: Adventures in Urban Anarchy*, London, Palgrave Macmillan.

Fisher, M. 2009. *Capitalist Realism: Is There No Alternative?* London, Zero Books.

Fiske, J. 1992. The Cultural Economy of Fandom. In *The Adorning Audience: Fan Culture and Popular Media*, Ed. L. Lewis, London, Routledge.

Foucault, M. 1977. *Discipline and Punish*, New York, NY, Pantheon.

Fred and Rose. 2014. [Film] Directed by R Anderson. s.l.: s.n.

Friedrich, J. 2002. *Der Brand: Deutschland im Bombenkrieg 1940–1945*, Berlin, Verlag Ullstein.

Fuller, M. 2017. Great Spatial Expectations: On Three Objects, Two Communities and One House, *Current Sociology*, 65(4), 603–622.

Fuller, M. and Löw, M. 2017. An Invitation to Spatial Sociology, *Current Sociology*, 65(4), 571–586.

Gieryn, T. 2000. A Space for Place in Sociology, *Annual Review of Sociology*, 26(1), 463–496.

Glaser, J., 2017. *What to Do with Confederate Statues?* [Online] Available at: https://theconversation.com/what-to-do-with-confederate-statues-81736 [Accessed 12 04 2018].

Graham, B., Ashworth, G. and Tunbridge, J. 2016. *A Geography of Heritage*, London, Routledge.

Grayling, A. 2006. *Among The Dead Cities: Is the Targeting of Civilians in War Ever Justified*, London, Bloomsbury.

Griffiths, J. 2017. *Thousands of People Visiting the Site of Fred and Rose West's House in Creepy Craze Where People Flock to Scenes of Murders and Disasters*. [Online] Available at: https://www.thesun.co.uk/living/2760998/thousands-of-people-visit-the-site-of-serial-killers-fred-and-rose-wests-house-due-to-rise-of-dark-tourism/ [Accessed 12 04 2018].

Gronlund, B. 1993. *Lefebvre's First Ontological Transformation of Space: Lived, Perceived and Conceived Space*, London, Routledge.

Hall, S. 2012. *Theorizing Crime and Deviance: A New Perspective*, London, Sage.

Hall, S. and Winlow, S. 2004. Barbarians at the Gate: Crime and Violence in the Breakdown of the Pseudo-Pacification Process. In *Cultural Criminology Unleashed*, Eds J. Ferrell K. Hayward W. Morrison and M. Presdee, London, Glasshouse Press.

Harvey, D. 1989. *The Condition of Postmodernity: An Enquiry into the Origins of Cultural Heritage*, Oxford, Blackwell.

Harvey, D. 2006. *Spaces of Global Capitalism*, London, Verso.

Harvey, D. 2012. *Rebel Cities*, London, Verso.

Harvey, D. (2015). Heritage and scale: settings, boundaries and relations. *International Journal of Heritage Studies*, 21(6), 577–593.

Hayward, K. 2004. Space -The Final Frontier: Criminology, the City and the Spatial Dynamics of Exclusion. In *Cultural Criminology Unleashed*, Eds J. Ferrell K. Hayward W. Morrison and M. Presdee, London, Glasshouse Press.

Hayward, K. 2012. Five Spaces of Cultural Criminology, *British Journal of Criminology*, 52(3), 441–462.

Herrup, C. 1989. *The Common Practice: Participation and the Criminal Law in Seventeenth-Century England*, Cambridge, Cambridge University Press.

HMSO. 1972. *City of York, South-West of the Ouse. An Inventory of the Historical Monuments in City of York*. [Online] Available at: http://www.british-history.ac.uk/rchme/york/vol3/xxix-xxxvi [Accessed 12 04 2018].

Hobsbawm, E. 2001. *Bandits*, London, Abacus.

Horkheimer, M. 1974. *Eclipse of Reason*, London, Seabury Press.

Huyssen, A. 1997. The Voids of Berlin, *Critical Inquiry*, 24(1), 57–81.

Jarvis, B. 2007. Monsters Inc.: Serial Killers and Consumer Culture, *Crime, Media, Culture*, 3(3), 326–344.

Jenks, C. and Lorentzen, J. 1997. The Kray Fascination, *Theory, Culture, Society*, 14(3), 87–107.

Jessop, B., Brenner, N. and Jones, M. 2008. Theorizing Sociospatial Relations, *Environment and Planning D: Society and Space*, 26(3), 389–401.

Knipe, W. 1867. *Criminal Chronology of York Castle; With a Register of the Criminals Capitally Convicted and Executed at the County Assizes*, London, Gale.

Knudsen, B. 2011. Thanatourism: Witnessing Difficult Pasts, *Tourist Studies*, 11(1), 55–72.

Kooistra, P. 1989. *Criminals as Heroes: Structure, Power & Identity*, Bowling Green, OH, Bowling Green State University Popular Press.

Lefebvre, H. 1991. *The Production of Space*, Oxford, Blackwell.

Lefebvre, H. 1996. *Writings on Cities*, Hoboken, NJ, Wiley.

Lefebvre, H. 2000a. *Critique of Everyday Life Volume 1*, New York, NY, Verso.

Lefebvre, H. 2000b. *Critique of Everyday Life Volume 2*, New York, NY, Verso.

Lefebvre, H. 2004. *Rhythmanalysis: Space, Time and Everyday Life*, London, Continuum.

Lefebvre, H. 2005. *Critique of Everyday Life Volume 3*, New York, NY, Verso.

Lefebvre, H. 2009. *State, Space, World: Selected Essays*, Minneapolis, MN, University of Minnesota Press.

Lennon, J. and Foley, M. 1996. *Dark Tourism*, London, Continuum.

Lennon, J. and Foley, M. n.d. *Dark Tourism*, London, Thompson.

Litter, J. 2005. British Heritage and the Legacies of Race. In *The Politics of Heritage: The Legacies of Race*, Eds J. Litter and R. Naidoo, Abingdon, Routledge.

Lloyd, S. 2017. *Dark Tourism: Working Title – Pilot.* [Online] Available at: https://www.youtube.com/watch?v= MKG8HUKueOY [Accessed 12 12 2017].

Logan, W. and Reeves, K. 2009. *Places of Pain and Shame: Dealing with 'Difficult Heritage'*, Abingdon, Routledge.

Lowenthal, L. 1961. *Literature, Popular Culture and Society*, Englewood Cliffs, NJ, Prentice-Hall.

Löw, M. and Weidenhaus, G. 2017. Borders that Relate: Conceptualizing Boundaries in Relational Space, *Current Sociology*, 65(4), 553–570.

Macdonald, P. 1995. *Independent*. [Online] Available at: http://www.independent.co.uk/life-style/life-what-to-do-with-a-house-of-horrors-1526451.html [Accessed 12 04 2018].

Macdonald, S. 1998. *The Politics of Display: Museums, Science, Culture*, London, Routledge.

Macdonald, S. 2006. Undesirable Heritage: Fascist Material Culture and Historical Consciousness in Nuremberg, *International Journal of Heritage Studies*, 12(1), 9–28.

Macdonald, S. 2009. *Difficult Heritage: Negotiating the Nazi Past in Nuremberg and Beyond*, London, Routledge.

Massey. 2013. *Space, Place and Gender*, Hoboken, NJ, John Wiley & Sons.

Massey, D. 1993. Power-Geometry and a Progressive Sense of Place. In *Mapping the Futures: Local Cultures, Global Change*, Eds L. Bondi et al., London, Routledge.

Massey, D. 1993. Power-Geometry and a Progressive Sense of Place. In *Mapping theFutures: Local Cultures, Global Change*, London, Routledge.

Massey, D. 2005. *For Space*, London, Sage.

McCorristine, S. 2014. *William Dcorder and the Red Barn Murder: Journeys of the Criminal Body*, Basingstoke, Palgrave Macmillan.

Mol, A. and Law, J. 1994. Regions, Networks and Fluids: Anaemia and Social Topology, *Social Studies of Science*, 24(4), 641–671.

Nieves, A. 2009. Places of Pain as Tools for Social Justice in the 'New South Africa': Black Heritage Preservation in the 'Rainbow' Nation's Townships. In *Places of Pain and Shame: Dealing with 'Difficult Heritage'*, Eds W. Logan and K. Reeves, Abingdon, Routledge.

Oakeshott, M. 1996. *The Politics of Faith and the Politics of Scepticism*, New Haven, CT, Yale University Press.

OpenStreetMap. 2017. *Map of South East York*. [Online] Available at: https://www.openstreetmap.org/search?query=york#map=17/53.94334/-1.10051 [Accessed 12 12 2017].

OrdnanceSurvey. 1853. *Yorkshire 174 South East, Six Inch England and Wales 1842–1952*, London, Ordnance Survey.

OrdnanceSurvey. 1910. *Yorkshire 174 South East, Six Inch England and Wales 1888–1913*, London, Ordnance Survey.

OrdnanceSurvey. 1932. *Yorkshire 174 South East, Six Inch England and Wales 1842–1952*, London, Ordnance Survey.

Parson, S. 1624. *The Plott of the Mannor of Dringhouses Lyinge Within the Countie of the Cittie of Yorke*, s.l.: City of York Council, York Archives.

Penfold-Mounce, R. 2010. *Celebrity Culture and Crime: The Joy of Transgression*, London, Palgrave Macmillan.

Penfold-Mounce, R. 2016. Corpses, Popular Culture and Forensic Science: Public Obsession with Death, *Mortality*, 21(1), 19–35.

Penfold-Mounce, R. 2018. *Death, The Dead and Popular Culture*, Bingley, Emerald Publishing.

Presdee, M. 2000. *Cultural Criminology and the Carnival of Crime*, London, Routledge.

Raymen, T. 2016. Designing-in Crime by Designing-out the Social? Situational Crime Prevention and the Intensification of Harmful Subjectivities, *British Journal of Criminology*, 56(3), 497–514.

Ritzer, G. 2003. Islands of the Living Dead: The Social Geography of McDonaldization, *American Behavioral Scientist*, 45(2), 119–136.

Ritzer, G. 2009. *McDonaldization: The Reader*, Newbury Park, CA, Pine Forge Press.

Ritzer, G. 2011. *The McDonaldization of Society*, London, Sage.

Rojek, C. 1993. *Ways of Escape*, Basingstoke, Palgrave Macmillan.

Seaton, A. 1996. Guided by the Dark: From Thanatopsis to Thanatourism, *International Journal of Heritage Studies*, 2(4), 234–244.

Sennett, R. 1977. *The Fall of Public Man*, London, Penguin.

Sharpley, R. 2009. Shedding Light on Dark Tourism: An Introduction. In *The Darker Side of Travel: The Theory and Practice of Dark Tourism*, Bristol, Channel View Publications.

Sharpley, R. and Stone, P. 2009. *The Darker Side of Travel: The Theory and Practice of Dark Tourism*, Bristol, Channel View Publications.

Sheller, M. 2017. From Spatial Turn to Mobilities Turn, *Current Sociology*, 623–639.

Shields, R. 1999. *Lefebvre, Love, and Struggle: Spatial Dialectics*, London, Routledge.

Shields, R. 2011. Henri Lefebvre. In *Key Thinkers on Space and Place*, Eds P. Hubbard and R. Kitchin, London, Sage.

Shipman, A. 2017. 'The Rise of Dark Tourism': Thousands Visit Spot Where Fred and Rose West's House of Death Once Stood. [Online] Available at: http://www.mirror.co.uk/news/weird-news/the-rise-dark-tourism-thousands-9730588 [Accessed 12 04 2018].

Sibley, D. 1995. *Geographies of Exclusion: Society and Difference in the West*, London, Routledge.

Simmel, G. 1905. *Kant: 16 Vorlesungen gehalten an der Berliner Universität*, München, Duncker Humboldt.

Simmel, G. 1908. The Stranger. In *Social Theory: The Multicultural and Classic Readings*, Ed Lemert, London, Routledge.

Simmel, G. 1997. The Sociology of Space. In *Simmel on Culture*, Eds D. Frisby and M. Featherstone, London, Sage.

Sotirakopolous, N. 2016. *The Rise of Lifestyle Activism: From New Left to Occupy*, London, Palgrave Macmillan.

Spokes, M. 2014. *The Contemporary Avant-Garde: Classification, Organization, Spatiality and Practices of Resistance*. PhD Thesis. [Online] Available at: http://etheses.

whiterose.ac.uk/8082/1/MSpokesYorkThesisSept2014.pdf [Accessed 12 04 2018].

Stone, P. 2006. A Dark Tourism Spectrum: Towards a Typology of Death and Macabre Related Tourist Sites, Attractions and Exhibitions, *Tourism: An Interdisciplinary, International Journal*, 52(2), 145–160.

Stone, P. 2009. Making Absent Death Present: Consuming Dark Tourism in Contemporary Society. In *The Darker Side of Travel: The Theory and Practice of Dark Tourism*, pp. 29–40. Bristol, Channel View Publications.

Stone, P. 2011. Dark Tourism: Towards a New Post-disciplinary Research Agenda, *International Journal of Tourism Anthropology*, 1(3/4), 318–332.

Stone, P., & Sharpley, R. (2008). Consuming dark tourism: a thanatological perspective. *Annals of Tourism Research*, 35(2), 574–595.

Strange, C. and Kempa, M. 2003. Shades of Dark Tourism: Alcatraz and Robben Island, *Annals of Tourism Research*, 30(2), 386–405.

Strathern, M. 2005. *Partial Connections*, Walnut Creek, CA, Rowman Altamira Press.

Tarlow, S. and Dyndor, Z. 2015. The Landscape of the Gibbet, *Landscape History*, 36(1), 71–88.

Taylor, F. 2008. *Death Toll Debate*. [Online] Available at: http://www.spiegel.de/international/germany/death-toll-debate-how-many-died-in-the-bombing-of-dresden-a-581992.html [Accessed 12 04 2018].

Thrift, N. 2003. Space. In *Key Concepts in Geography*, Eds S. Holloway S. Rice and G. Valentine, London, Sage.

Tillott, P. 1961. *Prisons and Gallows. In a History of the County of York: The City of York.* [Online] Available at: http://www.british-history.ac.uk/vch/yorks/city-of-york/pp491–498. http://www.british-history.ac.uk/vch/yorks/city-of-york/pp491–498#anchorn166. [Accessed 12 05 2017].

Tunbridge, J., & Ashworth, G. (1996). *Dissonant Heritage: the Management of the Past as a Resource in Conflict.* New York, NY: John Wiley & Sons.

Utaka, Y. 2009. The Hiroshima 'Peace Memorial': Transforming Legacy, Memories and Landscapes. In *Places of Pain and Shame: Dealing with 'Difficult Heritage'*, Eds W. Logan and K. Reeves, Abingdon, Routledge.

von Borries, B. 2015. Kommunikative und kulturelle Dimension der Erinnerung an den Nationalsozialismus. Die vierte Generation als Umschlag?! In *Erinnern wozu? Beiträge zur politisch-historischen Bildung*, Ed U. Hirschfield, Berlin, LIT Verlag.

Waterton, E. and Watson, S. 2013. Framing Theory: Towards a Critical Imagination in Heritage Studies, *International Journal of Heritage Studies*, 19(6), 546–551.

Watkins, C. 2005. Representations of Space, Spatial Practices and Spaces of Representation: an Application of Lefebvre's Spatial Triad, *Culture and Organization*, 11(3), 209–220.

Webber, R. and Burrows, R. 2016. Life in the Alpha Territory: Discontinuity and Conflict in an Elite London 'Village', *Urban Studies*, 35(15), 3139–3154.

Willis, E. 2014. *Theatricality, Dark Tourism and Ethical Spectatorship: Absent Others*, London, Palgrave Macmillan.

Winlow, S., Hall, S., Briggs, D. and Treadwell, J. 2015. *Riots and Political Protest*, London, Routledge.

Winlow, S., Hall, S. and Treadwell, J. 2017. *The Rise of the Right: English Nationalism and the Transformation of Working-Class Politics*, Bristol, Policy Press.

Winter, T. 2014. Heritage Studies and the Privileging of Theory, *International Journal of Heritage Studies*, 20(5), 556–572.

Woodrow, J. 2012. *Rose West: The Making of a Monster*, London, Hodder Paperbacks.

Yeoh, S. 2017. The World Class City, the Homeless and the Soup Kitchens of Kuala, *Current Sociology*, 65(4), 571–586.

Young, K. 2009. Auschwitz-Birkenau: The Challenges of Heritage Management Following the Cold War. In *Places of Pain and Shame: Dealing with 'Difficult Heritage'*, Eds W. Logan and K. Reeves, Abingdon, Routledge.

Zierold, M. 2008. Memory and Media Cultures. In *Cultural Memory Studies: An International and Interdisciplinary Handbook*, Eds A. Erll and A. Nünning, Berlin, Walter de Gruyter.

INDEX

Absent-present paradox, 101–102
Alcatraz, 6
Anticipated experience, 99
Anti-memorialization, 81, 88, 92, 97, 99, 133–134
'Arbeit Macht Frei' gate, Auschwitz, 4–5
Audience, as media viewers, 98
Auschwitz, 16–17
  'Arbeit Macht Frei' gate, 4–5
Auschwitz-Birkenau, 16
Authorized heritage discourses (AHD), 18

Barbarism of order, 118, 122, 127
Black spots, 6
Bodily punishment, 40
'Bomb Dome, A' (Hiroshima), 3–4
Brady, Ian, 93

Chapman, Jessica, 83

China
  Tibetan Buddhist monasteries, removal of, 90
Commodification, 92
Conceived space, 34
  Dresden's Neumarkt as, 109–115
  Number 25 Cromwell Street as, 88–92
  Tyburn as, 37–48
Concept-city, 108, 111
Consumption, 10, 79–105
  space of, 102–104
  see also Number 25 Cromwell Street (Gloucester)
Container space, 112–114, 119, 120
Contradictory space, 10, 81, 83, 86, 136
  theatrical space as, 99–102
Corr, Jimmy, 76
Creative thinking, 19
Criminal-celebrity, 2, 5, 6, 93
Criminal fan, 6

Critical imagination, 25, 132
Cycle crossing, 73

Dahmer, Jeffrey, 83
Daily reality, 35, 57, 87
Dark tourism, 5–8, 81, 91, 93, 99, 136, 137
  research, 3, 5
  theorists, 1
Dark Tourism (documentary), 101
Death, 7–8
Demolition, 4
Denazification, 128
Deviant spaces, 7–8
Dick's gravestone in St. George's Churchyard, 50
Difficult heritage, 1–4, 6–8, 10–12, 15–18, 25, 101, 107, 114, 134–136
Distance markers of the road, 54
Dramatic action of the space, 67–68, 128
  fictitious counterparts, 68–69, 71–72, 97–98
  real counterparts, 69–72, 97–98
Dringhouses, 28

Embodiment, 23, 25
England
  race heritage, 3
  spaces of memorialization, 7

Fenced-off saplings, 58, 59
Forgetting, 91
Frauenkirche, 110

Germany
  National Democratic Party, 108
  Neumarkt, Dresden, 6, 11, 107–129
  spaces of memorialization, 7
  swastika-laden ceilings, Nuremburg, 1
Globalization, 14, 18
  socioeconomic ramifications of, 23–24
Gloucester Council, 80, 82, 84, 89, 90, 94, 97, 135
Grassland, 59, 60
Ground Zero, 16

Heritage, 3–6
  architecture, 2, 4, 89
  building, 4
  difficult, 1–4, 6–8, 10–12, 15–18, 25, 101, 107, 114, 134–136
  violent, 6
Hindley, Myra, 93
Hiroshima, 6
  'A Bomb Dome', 3–4
Hob Stone, 54, 55
Hot spots, 111

Huntley, Ian, 83

Informal pathway, 62–65
Interpretive experience, 99

Jacobite rebellion of 1745, 39, 69–70
John Thornton Memorial Plaque, 70–72

Kilburn High Road, 16, 27–77
Kuala Lumpur, 24

Lefebvre's spatial triad, 8–11, 13, 19, 22–25, 29–37, 66–68, 80–81, 108, 110, 131–132
Leisure space, 60–62
Liminality, in contested spaces, 37
Little Hob Moor, 66
 cycle route across, 53
 noticeboard, 51–52, 53
Lived space, 34–35
 Number 25 Cromwell Street as, 92–96
 Tyburn as, 48–57
Lizzie Borden Bed and Breakfast Museum, 83
Localism, 18
Lord Mayor, 38
Lund's Inclosures Act map of 1772, 58

Materialisation, 92
May 1968 uprising, Paris, 34
McDonaldization phenomenon, 120
Media coverage, 81
Medieval boundary stone, 51, 52
Memorialization, 2, 7–8, 19
Mind research, 2
Monetization of the dead, 2
Murderabilia, 84, 92
Museums, 5

National Democratic Party of Germany (NPD), 108
Network-based approaches, 14
Neumarkt, Dresden, 6, 11, 107–129, 134
 as conceived space, 109–115
 as perceived space, 115–122
 spatial practice and political subjectivities, 122–126
Number 25 Cromwell Street (Gloucester), 6, 10, 16, 79–105, 133–134
 as conceived space, 88–92
 as lived space, 92–96

as perceived space, 87–88
as theatrical space, 96–99
Nuremberg Documentation Centre, 5
Nuremburg, Germany, 16
swastika-laden ceilings, 1
One-dimensionalism, 14

Paris
  May 1968 uprising, 34
PEGIDA, 11
Perceived space, 35
  Dresden's Neumarkt as, 115–122
  Number 25 Cromwell Street as, 87–88
  Tyburn as, 57–65
Performance, 65
Physical spaces, 22
Place-based approaches, 14
Plague Stone Plaque, 54–56
Planting of new saplings, 58
Poland
  heritage, 4
Political subjectivities, 122–126
Politicization, 10–11, 107–129
  see also Neumarkt, Dresden
Politics of display, 4, 84
Power, 15–19
Power geometry, 18, 25

Preservation, 4
Public good, 119

Quality of life, 119

Relationality of space, 20–21, 23
Representations of space *see* Conceived space
Rhythm analysis, 104, 132
'Right to the City', 25
Robertson Bell Associates, 84–85

Scale, 15–19
Scale-based approaches, 14
Secure zones, 111
Semperoper, 110
Social centrality, 23
Sociality of space, 21–22, 23, 33
South Africa
  black heritage in, 3
Space
  conceived, 34, 37–48, 88–92, 109–115
  contradictory, 10, 81, 83, 86, 99–102, 136
  Lefebvre's spatial triad, 8–11, 13, 19, 22–25, 29–37
  leisure, 60–62
  lived, 34–35, 48–57, 92–96
  perceived, 35, 57–65, 87–88, 115–122
  as relational, 20–21
  as social, 21–22, 33

theatrical, 9–10, 27–77, 96–102
Spatial practice, 122–126
Spatial purification, 119
Spatial theorists, 2
Swastika-laden ceilings, Nuremburg, Germany, 1
Symbolic spaces, 22

Territorial approaches, 14
Thanatourism, 5, 6, 15, 16
Theatrical space, 9–10, 27–77
  as contradictory space, 99–102
  Lefebvre's spatial triad, 31–37
  Number 25 Cromwell Street as, 96–99
  Tyburn as, 65–76
  see also Tyburn, York
Thornton, John, 76
Thought, 34
Three Legged Mare, 50, 51
Time–space compression, 16
Turkey
  Armenian churches, demolition of, 90
Turpin, Richard 'Dick', 98, 133
Tyburn, York, 6, 16, 17, 27–77, 132–133, 135
  contemporary map, 41, 46, 47

cycle crossing, 73
cycle route across Little Hob Moor, 53
detail, 27–28
Dick's gravestone in St. George's Churchyard, 50
distance markers of the road, 54
fenced-off saplings, 58, 59
floral tributes, 29, 30
grassland, 59, 60
as historically and topographically conceived space, 37–48
Hob Stone, 54, 55
informal pathway, 62–65
information sign, 47, 48
leisure space, 60–62
Little Hob Moor noticeboard, 51–52, 53
as lived space, 48–57
medieval boundary stone, 51, 52
Ordnance Survey map, 41–45
Parson's 1624 map, 39–41
as perceived space, 57–65
Plague Stone Plaque, 54–56
planting of new saplings, 58

reverse angle, 77
site with bench, 47, 49
surrounding woodland, 28, 29
as theatrical space, 65–76
Three Legged Mare, 50, 51
see also Theatrical space

Urban containers, 112–114, 120
Urban reality, 35, 57, 60–62, 87

Urban space, 23

Violent heritage, 6

West, Fred, 83–84, 95–96, 107
West, Rose, 84, 95–96, 107
Wooded space, 57
Woodland Trust, 58
Woodthorpe, 28

York City Council, 28, 135